Oxford Reading Tree

Stories for Writing

Teaching Handbook

Age 4–5

Created by
Pie Corbett

Teaching Handbook written by
Charlotte Raby and Pie Corbett

OXFORD
UNIVERSITY PRESS

OXFORD
UNIVERSITY PRESS

Great Clarendon Street, Oxford OX2 6DP

Oxford University Press is a department of the University of Oxford.
It furthers the University's objective of excellence in research, scholarship,
and education by publishing worldwide

First published 2010

Page make-up and additional artwork by Oxford Designers and Illustrators

Acknowledgements

Rosie's Walk

Original edition first published in English by Random House
Children's Books, a division of The Random House Group Ltd

Copyright © Patricia Hutchins, 1968

The right of Pat Hutchins to be identified as the author of this work has been
asserted in accordance with the Copyright, Designs and Patents Act 1988.

All extracts on following pages by kind permission of Random House
Children's Books and copyright © Patricia Hutchins, 1968: p23, p27

You Choose

Original edition first published in English by Random House
Children's Books, a division of The Random House Group Ltd

Text © Pippa Goodhart 2003
Illustrations © Nick Sharratt 2003

The right of Pippa Goodhart/Nick Sharratt to be identified as the
author/illustrator of this work has been asserted in accordance with
the Copyright, Designs and Patents Act 1988.

All extracts on following pages by kind permission of Random House
Children's Books and copyright Text © Pippa Goodhart 2003,
Illustrations © Nick Sharratt 2003: p23, p35

My Brother

Original edition first published in English by Random House
Children's Books, a division of The Random House Group Ltd

Copyright © AET Browne, 2007

The right of Anthony Browne to be identified as the author of this work has been
asserted in accordance with the Copyright, Designs and Patents Act 1988.

All extracts on following pages by kind permission of Random House Children's
Books and copyright © AET Browne, 2007: p6, p23, p43

www.OxfordPrimary.co.uk

ISBN: 978-0-19-911944-8

1 3 5 7 9 10 8 6 4 2

Printed in Great Britain by Ashford Colour Press

Contents

A letter from Pie Corbett

Dear colleague,

Welcome to *Stories for Writing* for the early years, featuring the following favourite picture books: *Rosie's Walk* by Pat Hutchins, *My Brother* by Anthony Browne and *You Choose* by Nick Sharratt and Pippa Goodhart.

These are just three of my favourite picture books and I have chosen them for *Stories for Writing* to incorporate my unique teaching system based on *Talk for Writing* to support storytelling, reading comprehension and writing in the classroom at Key Stage 1/P1–3.

If you follow the Stories for Writing teaching process and take advantage of the cross-curricular and extended writing activities that accompany every story book, there is between 4–6 weeks worth of teaching materials for every story. However, as with any quality resource, this is flexible and you should feel comfortable to adapt my ideas to suit your teaching.

The Age 4–5 materials include:

- A **CD-ROM** with three interactive picture books on screen, videos of me telling my version of the story and an editable story map
- A **Planning CD-ROM** with editable lesson plans, teaching ideas and cross-curricular activities
- Special educational editions of the **picture books** for use in group/guided and independent reading sessions with inside cover notes for use in the classroom and at home
- This **Teaching Handbook**, with step-by-step guidance for every story, so that you can follow the teaching and learning sequence, including a wealth of photocopiable Resource Sheets for group and independent work

I would love to hear your experiences of using *Stories for Writing* with your children. Do come and meet me at one of my events, if you haven't already, or e-mail me to let me know how you get on. My email address is **pie@oup.com** or check out **www.OxfordPrimary.co.uk/StoriesforWriting** to find out more.

Good luck and have fun unlocking the power of storytelling in your classroom!

Best wishes,

Pie Corbett

Pie Corbett
Talk for Writing **expert and creator of** *Stories for Writing*

Unlock the power of storytelling

Storytelling is at the heart of every culture. Good stories echo in the mind, acting as the blueprint for creativity and for understanding the world we live in. It is impossible to create a story out of nothing – experience of reading quality picture books, coupled with memorable storytelling, is an effective way of developing a child's imaginative world. *Stories for Writing* provides this bridge for children.

READING A STORY

Storytelling starts with the children experiencing the pleasure of a quality picture book. The class loiter with the story, discussing what happens as well as exploring and building the story's world through drama, model-making and art work. Constant rereading makes the book memorable and helps the children to internalise the language patterns. The foundations of reading are then built upon by listening to, joining in with and learning to tell another story based on the book's patterns and themes.

RETELLING A STORY

Oral storytelling is supported by a multi-sensory approach. A story map provides a visual reminder whilst actions support kinaesthetic learning, making key language patterns memorable and meaningful. The children keep retelling the tale together until they are ready to retell in groups and pairs. Revisiting the story over a number of days ensures that everyone can retell it.

CREATING A STORY

Once the oral story is deeply embedded in the children's 'story bank', the class move on to creating their own version. The old story map is annotated, changes and embellishments made, as a new class story emerges. The new story can be retold orally before the teacher uses shared writing to capture and craft it, with children's assistance. The teacher then supports the children to draw new maps, using their own ideas. They retell their own stories with a partner until their tale has been crafted and honed. The final stage is for the children to write or record their stories.

This story bridge means that when the children write, they are basing their story on both the original book and oral retelling. It is this gradual and memorable approach that ensures every child develops their own story.

Stories for Writing teaching sequence

TALKING AND READING

TALK

1 **Talk together**

- Use the Talk questions to tune the children into the book they are about to read by linking to children's wider knowledge and raising their curiosity.

> **TALK**
>
> - Before reading the book, talk about the choices the children made this morning.
> - *What did they have for breakfast? What did they choose to bring to school? What book did they choose to read this morning?*
>
> Use Resource Sheet 1 on page 60 for the children to draw their choices.

READ

2 **Share the story on screen**

- Enjoy reading the storybook together on the interactive whiteboard.
- Use the Book Talk questions to explore the story in detail, imaginatively entering the story world.

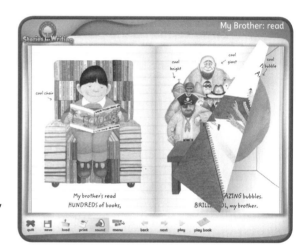

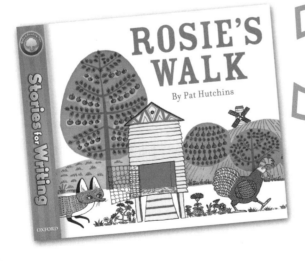

3 **Read the picture books**

- Immerse children in the story in group/guided reading sessions to deepen understanding and enjoyment.
- Encourage children to share the book at home.
- Retell the story in the children's own words using the instructions in this handbook.

Resource Sheets

Photocopiable Resource Sheets to accompany every story are highlighted throughout the teaching notes to support children's storytelling, reading comprehension and writing.

Pie Corbett's 6 steps to success!

STORYTELLING AND WRITING

TELL

4

Tell a new story with Pie

- Watch the video of Pie telling his new story, based on the original story idea and patterns.

- Join in telling the new story with Pie using his actions and story map.

- As children become more confident, tell the story without Pie as a class, in groups, pairs and independently.

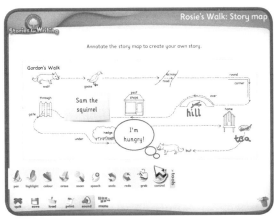

WRITE

5

Write a class story

- Plan a new class story using the editable story map on the CD-ROM.

- Write the shared class story using the instructions in this handbook. Turn this into a class Big Book or a wall story.

Children write their own stories

6

- Children create their own story maps and retell their new story.

- Children now write or record their own stories, using the shared and guided sessions as a scaffold.

Cross-curricular and Extended Writing support

Cross-curricular and Extended Writing ideas are included in the teaching notes for every story and can be integrated into your teaching at any point. These help children understand the story and inhabit the story world.

The *Stories for Writing* components

With the *Stories for Writing* CD-ROM you and the children can:

Read and share the story on screen

Listen to the story being read

Interact with the story using the interactive tool bar

Display and edit the story maps for each book to prepare children for telling and writing their own story

Watch Pie Corbett telling his version of the story and join in with him

In the *Stories for Writing* picture books you will find:

Guidance for parents and carers on how to share the book at home on the inside front cover

Ideas for reading and sharing the story during group/guided and independent reading sessions on the inside back cover

Notes about the author and illustrator for each story

Notes from Pie Corbett explaining why he chose the story

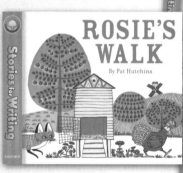

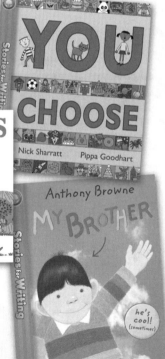

With the *Stories for Writing* **Teaching Handbook** you will find:

Step-by-step guidance for every storybook, showing how to incorporate Pie Corbett's *Stories for Writing* teaching process into your classroom

A wealth of photocopiable Resource Sheets to support children's storytelling, reading comprehension and writing

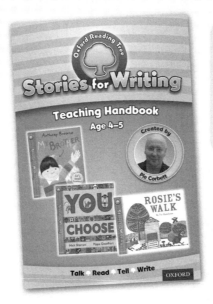

Advice for assessing children's writing

Exciting cross-curricular teaching ideas

Topic links to Oxford Reading Tree classic storybooks

The *Stories for Writing* **Planning CD-ROM** contains:

Printable weekly lesson plans using the Oxford Planning Tools

The ability to edit, adapt and save your own planning and resources

Support for cross-curricular teaching

Extra Resource Sheets – perfect for Take Home!

Ideas for mixed-age planning

Progression in *Stories for Writing*

All children need a bank of stories to draw on when creating their own. By engaging with the story; listening to it on screen; reading in pairs, in group and guided reading and at home; through exploration of character, setting and language; through role-play and drama, all children can enjoy and internalise stories.

Progression in *Stories for Writing* comes through the way the children interact with the story. This is broken up into four levels:

All ages

Imitate

The children loiter with the storybook until they are very familiar with the language patterns and have throughly entered the story's imaginative world. Use a copy of the story map for children to retell the story in their own words and pick up on familiar language patterns.

Age 4–5/Reception/P1

Simple patterned innovation

The Reception stories are retold as **simple patterned innovations** so that the children get to practise making simple changes to a story. These changes give the children ownership of the storytelling, whilst the repetitive structure of the original stories gives them the security to try out their own ideas. Encourage children to create their own stories, drawing a map. Try out the changes as a class and group retelling before the children have a go at independent retelling and writing.

Age 5–6/Year 1/P2

Complex innovation

The Year 1 stories are innovated in Pie's storytelling video. He changes characters, adds details and alters the story. The original story structure or idea remains but the children move from a simple repetitive patterned retelling to more fluent prose. Work together to create innovated class stories to retell. Encourage children to create their own stories, drawing story maps before they attempt independent retelling and writing.

Age 6–7/Year 2/P3
Invent

In Year 2 the children are focused on telling stories and using the writer's craft. The stories they explore give them the basis for creating their own adventures, characters and settings. The invented story told by Pie in his video shows the children how each story can be used to create a new one. By Year 2, children create their own stories, based on the original story idea, but craft the tale individually, drawing on the storybook as well as Pie's oral version.

Assessment in *Stories for Writing* (Age 4–5)

Formative assessment is essential in identifying the gaps in children's learning and working out how to move their reading and writing on. The *Stories for Writing* process gives children plenty of time to practise and internalise story language and structures so that by the time they record their story they can concentrate on the writer's craft.

Specific reading and writing skills are addressed through partner talk and the use of mini whiteboards in the **shared writing** sessions. **Guided reading** and **guided writing** sessions are the best place to *jump into* the reading and writing process and focus on the area that the children need more input on. Use the differentiated guided writing activities, which link to the shared writing focus, to move a group of children's writing on.

ASSESSING CHILDREN'S WRITING AND READING

The Teaching Handbook gives guidance on how to assess children's writing against a specific Assessment Focus. You will find advice on what to look for in the children's writing and ideas for moving them on, as well as suggested Assessment Scale Points to help you assess the children's reading proficiency for each book.

The following chart gives an overview of the Assessment Scale points suggested for Reception/P1 for each storybook.

Picture book	Assessment Scale Points (Writing)	Assessment Scale Points (Reading)
Rosie's Walk	**EYF CCL Reading scale point 7**: Retells narratives in the correct sequence drawing on language patterns of stories.	**EYF CCL Reading scale point 4**: Knows that, in English, print is read from left to right and top to bottom. **EYF CCL Reading scale point 5**: Shows an understanding of the elements of stories, such as main character, sequence of events and openings. **EYF CCL Reading scale point 7**: Re-tells narratives in the correct sequence, drawing on language patterns of stories.
You Choose	**EYF CCL Writing scale point 6**: Attempts writing for a variety of purposes using features of different forms.	**EYF CCL Reading scale point 5**: Shows an understanding of the elements of stories, such as main character, sequence of events and openings. **EYF CCL Reading scale point 7**: Re-tells narratives in the correct sequence, drawing on language patterns of stories.
My Brother	**EYF CCL Writing scale point 8**: Begins to use captions and simple sentences sometimes using punctuation.	**EYF CCLReading scale point 4**: Knows that, in English, print is read from left to right and top to bottom. **EYF CCL Reading scale point 5**: Shows an understanding of the elements of stories, such as main character, sequence of events and openings. **EYF CCL Reading scale point 7**: Re-tells narratives in the correct sequence, drawing on language patterns of stories.

Planning with *Stories for Writing*

The *Stories for Writing* **Planning CD-ROM** provides you with a set of editable weekly plans for each picture book, accompanied by extra Resource Sheets and cross-curricular ideas to enrich the children's reading and writing experience. It uses all the teaching ideas in the *Teaching Handbook* and provides you with a structure for your teaching that can be adapted to suit you and your children's needs.

The **Planning CD-ROM** also includes advice and suggestions for using *Stories for Writing* in a mixed-age setting.

For each book, the **Planning CD-ROM** contains:

> **A Unit overview:** a summary of the six-week teaching plan with links to the Early Years Foundation Stage objectives and the Scottish Curriculum for Excellence, assessment focuses, outcomes and cross-curricular ideas
>
> **Six Unit plans:** differentiated teaching ideas and take-home activities in step-by-step plans that can be printed out for an at-a-glance teaching prompt
>
> **Cross-curricular ideas:** exciting ideas for teaching across the wider curriculum
>
> **Resource Sheets:** an extensive set of extra Literacy and Cross-curricular activity sheets for use in the classroom or to take home

You can access all these materials through the software's easy navigation tools. The drop-down menus will allow you to select the plans you require, Resource Sheets and cross-curricular teaching ideas for each book in a few easy steps.

An example plan

Here is an example of a unit of work from the *Stories for Writing*
Planning CD-ROM, based on the picture book *My Brother.*

Stories for Writing headings
show the stage of the process
to be covered in each session

Suggestions for activities
children can do at home

Session	Objectives	Summary	Starter	Main teaching	Group or Independent work (Activity with ideas for differentiation where appropriate)	Plenary	Take-home activity
1 Talk	CLL Language for communication 14: Have confidence to speak to others about their own wants and interests.	Talk about families.	Talk about your family, and who is the oldest and youngest of any siblings. Describe a family activity.	Get the children to talk about their family and the activities they enjoy doing together.	Use Resource Sheet 1 for children to draw a picture of themselves with their family. *Add pictures of pets or activities. **Write names from memory as labels.	Show the cover of the book *My Brother*. Talk about the boy. *Would you like to meet this boy? What is he doing?*	Children may want to take home a clean copy of Resource Sheet 1 and draw a picture of their family at an event, or their family pets.
2 Read (Read the story together)	CLL Language for communication 7: Sustain attentive listening, responding to what they have heard with relevant comments, questions or actions.	Talk about and read the book.	Show the front cover of the book on the screen. Read the title and talk about it.	Listen to the story all the way through. Encourage children to join in with the reading. Share personal responses, asking for children's questions and observations.	Start **guided reading groups** (notes can be found on the inside back cover of the book). *Listen to the story a second time. **Write a response to *My Brother* (Resource Sheet 2) now.	Look at the labels on page 3. Ask the children to find the word that is used most often. *Can they link each sound to the correct letters in 'cool'? Encourage the children to attempt to sound out more difficult words, such as 'sandals'.*	
3 Read (Book talk)	CLL Language for thinking 5: Use talk to organize, sequence and clarify thinking, ideas, feelings and events.	Talk about the book and respond to it.	Look through the book on screen. Focus on the page where the boy is flying. Talk about how text goes from left to right, but the text on this page goes up too. *Why? Is it a clever idea?*	Re-read the story on screen, stopping at different pages to ask the Book talk questions. Encourage the children to join in with the reading and ask their own questions about the book too. Share their responses.	**Guided reading group** Encourage personal responses to *My Brother* (Resource Sheet 2). *Should have adult support **Have a go at writing words to replace 'cool'.	Write extra labels for some of the pictures, e.g. for the animals. Ask the children to help you check your spelling. Encourage them to sound out the letters and blend to check the spelling is correct.	
4 Read (Explore the story)	CLL Reading 1: Show an understanding of the elements of stories, such as main character, sequence of events and openings.	Look at setting and character.	Zoom in on the hidden elephants under the jumping boy. Follow the setting activity in the *Teaching Handbook*.	Zoom in on the lady and gorilla and discuss the Setting questions. Zoom in on the bully and monster and discuss the Characters questions.	**Guided group work** *The children use Resource Sheet 3 to think about other settings for the climb, then discuss in pairs **Children can use Resource Sheet 4 to think of (and write) labels using adjectives.	Can the children think of adjectives to describe the animals in the book?	
5 Read (Explore the story)	CLL Language for communication 15: Extend their vocabulary, exploring the meanings and sounds of new words.	Focus on adjectives.	Play: What's in the box?	Re-read the book, focusing on the adjectives. Focus model using adjectives to describe one of the pictures.	**Guided group work** *Focus on one page and use adjectives to describe what they see. ** Children think of alternative adjectives to describe the same thing.	Children can play Who is it? by describing a character in the book. The others guess who it is.	Children play 'What is it?', describing an object for someone at home to guess.

Literacy objectives provide
a focus for each session

Prompts for whole class, group and independent
work, so you can get the most out of the
materials and resources. One-star and two-star
activities help you to support children to work at
their own level

Objectives Chart for *Rosie's Walk*

This chart shows the Early Years Foundation Stage and Scottish Curriculum for Excellence objectives that can be covered using the teaching notes for *Rosie's Walk* (pages 26 to 33) and the detailed planning grids on the Planning CD-ROM. The Planning CD-ROM shows how the teaching breaks down into six units of work, with five sessions in each unit.

Unit	Stories for Writing	Early Years Foundation Stage objectives
1	Talk Read	**CLL Language for thinking 5**: Use talk to organise, sequence and clarify thinking, ideas, feelings and events. **CLL Language for communication 10**: Listen with enjoyment and respond to stories, songs and other music, rhymes and poem s and make up their own. **CLL Reading 1**: Show an understanding of the elements of stories, such as main character, sequence of events, etc. **CLL Reading 2**: Know that print carries meaning and, in English, is read from left to right and top to bottom.
2	Read Tell	**CLL Language for thinking 2**: Use language to imagine and recreate roles and experiences. **CLL Reading 1**: Show an understanding of the elements of stories, such as main character, sequence of events etc. **CLL Linking sounds and letters 2**: Link sounds to letters, naming and sounding the letters of the alphabet. **CLL Reading 3**: Re-tell narratives in the correct sequence, drawing on language patterns of stories. **CLL Language for thinking 5**: Use talk to organise, sequence and clarify thinking, ideas, feelings and events.
3	Tell Write	**CLL Reading 3**: Re-tell narratives in the correct sequence, drawing on language patterns of stories. **CLL Writing 2**: Attempt writing for different purposes, using features of different forms such as lists, stories and instructions. **CLL Language for thinking 5**: Use talk to organise, sequence and clarify thinking, ideas, feelings and events.
4	Write	**CLL Reading 3**: Re-tell narratives in the correct sequence, drawing on language patterns of stories. **CLL Language for thinking 5**: Use talk to organise, sequence and clarify thinking, ideas, feelings and events. **CLL Reading 1**: Show an understanding of the elements of stories, such as main character, sequence of events, etc. **CLL Writing 2**: Attempt writing for different purposes, using features of different forms such as lists, stories and instructions.
5	Write	**CLL Writing 2**: Attempt writing for different purposes, using features of different forms such as lists, stories and instructions. **CLL Reading 3**: Re-tell narratives in the correct sequence, drawing on language patterns of stories. **CLL Language for communication 12**: Speak clearly and audibly with confidence and control and show awareness of the listener. **CLL Language for communication 6**: Interact with others, negotiating plans and activities and taking turns in conversation. **CLL Language for thinking 5**: Use talk to organise, sequence and clarify thinking, ideas, feelings and events.
6	Extended Writing	**CLL Language for thinking 2**: Use language to imagine and recreate roles and experiences. **CLL Writing 2**: Attempt writing for different purposes, using features of different forms such as lists, stories and instructions. **CLL Reading 1**: Show an understanding of ... how information can be found in non-fiction texts to answer questions about where, who, why and how. **CLL Writing 3**: Write their own names and other things such as labels and captions, and begin to form simple sentences, sometimes using punctuation.

Unit	*Stories for Writing*	Scottish Curriculum for Excellence objectives
1	Talk Read	**LIT 0-07a** To help me understand stories and other texts, I ask questions and link what I am learning with what I already know. **LIT 0-01b** I enjoy exploring and choosing stories and other texts to watch, read and listen to, and can share my likes and dislikes. **LIT 0-16a** To help me understand stories and other texts, I ask questions and link what I am learning with what I already know. **LIT 0-19a** I enjoy exploring events and characters in stories and other texts, sharing my thoughts in different ways. **ENG 0-12a** I explore sounds, letters and words, discovering how they work together, and I can use what I learn to help me as I read and write.
2	Read Tell	**LIT 0-19a** I enjoy exploring events and characters in stories and other texts, sharing my thoughts in different ways. **ENG 0-12a** I explore sounds, letters and words, discovering how they work together, and I can use what I learn to help me as I read and write. **LIT 0-11b** I enjoy exploring and choosing stories and other texts to watch, read and listen to, and can share my likes and dislikes. **LIT 0-01c** I enjoy exploring events and characters in stories and other texts, sharing my thoughts in different ways.
3	Tell Write	**LIT 0-07a** To help me understand stories and other texts, I ask questions and link what I am learning with what I already know. **LIT 0-01c** I enjoy exploring events and characters in stories and other texts, sharing my thoughts in different ways. **ENG 0-31a** I enjoy exploring events and characters in stories and other texts and I use what I learn to invent my own, sharing these with others in imaginative ways. **LIT 0-20a** I enjoy exploring and playing with the patterns and sounds of language and can use what I learn. **LIT 0-21b** As I play and learn, I enjoy exploring interesting materials for writing and different ways of recording my experiences and feelings, ideas and information.
4	Write	**LIT 0-21b** As I play and learn, I enjoy exploring interesting materials for writing and different ways of recording my experiences and feelings, ideas and information. **LIT 0-31a** I enjoy exploring events and characters in stories and other texts and I use what I learn to invent my own, sharing these with others in imaginative ways. **LIT 0-21a** I explore sounds, letters and words, discovering how they work together, and I can use what I learn to help me as I read or write. **LIT 0-26a** Within real and imaginary situations, I share experiences and feelings, ideas and information in a way that communicates my message.
5	Write	**LIT 0-21a** I explore sounds, letters and words, discovering how they work together, and I can use what I learn to help me as I read or write. **LIT 0-20a** I enjoy exploring and playing with the patterns and sounds of language and can use what I learn. **LIT 0-31a** I enjoy exploring events and characters in stories and other texts and I use what I learn to invent my own, sharing these with others in imaginative ways. **LIT 0-02a** As I listen and talk in different situations, I am learning to take turns and am developing my awareness of when to talk and when to listen. **LIT 0-04a** I listen or watch for useful or interesting information and I use this to make choices or learn new things. **LIT 0-14a** I use signs, books or other texts to find useful or interesting information and I use this to plan, make choices or learn new things.
6	Extended Writing	**LIT 0-01c** I enjoy exploring events or characters in stories and other texts, sharing my thoughts in different ways. **LIT 0-21b** As I play and learn, I enjoy exploring interesting materials for writing and different ways of recording my experiences and feelings, ideas and information. **LIT 0-16a** To help me understand stories and other texts, I ask questions and link what I am learning with what I already know. **LIT 0-21a** I explore sounds, letters and words, discovering how they work together, and I can use what I learn to help me as I read or write. **LIT 0-20a** I enjoy exploring and playing with the patterns and sounds of language and can use what I learn.

Objectives Chart for *You Choose*

This chart shows the Early Years Foundation Stage and Scottish Curriculum for Excellence objectives that can be covered using the teaching notes for *You Choose* (pages 34 to 41) and the detailed planning grids on the Planning CD-ROM. The Planning CD-ROM shows how the teaching breaks down into six units of work, with five sessions in each unit.

Unit	*Stories for Writing*	Early Years Foundation Stage objectives
1	Talk Read	**CLL Language for communication 14:** Have confidence to speak to others about their own wants and interests. **CLL Language for communication 7:** Sustain attentive listening… **CLL Reading 7:** Explore and experiment with sounds, words and texts. **CLL Language for communication 8:** Enjoy listening to and using spoken and written language, and readily turn to it in their play and learning. **CLL Language for thinking 2:** Use language to imagine and recreate roles and experiences.
2	Read Tell	**CLL Language for thinking 2:** Use language to imagine and recreate roles and experiences. **CLL Reading 1:** Show an understanding of the element of stories such as main character, etc. **CLL Linking sounds and letters 3:** Use their phonic knowledge to write simple regular words and make phonetically plausible attempts at more complex words. **CLL Reading 3:** Re-tell narratives in the correct sequence, drawing on language patterns of stories. **CLL Language for communication 15:** Extend their vocabulary, exploring the meanings and sounds of new words. **CLL Language for thinking 5:** Use talk to organise, sequence and clarify thinking, ideas, feelings and events.
3	Tell Write	**CLL Reading 3:** Re-tell narratives in the correct sequence, drawing on language patterns of stories. **CLL Language for thinking 5:** use talk to organise, sequence and clarify thinking, ideas, feelings and events. **CLL Writing 2:** Attempt writing for different purposes, using features of different forms such as lists, stories and instructions. **CLL Language for communication 6:** Interact with others, negotiating plans and activities and taking turns in conversation.
4	Write	**CLL Reading 3:** Re-tell narratives in the correct sequence, drawing on the language patterns of stories. **CLL Language for thinking 5:** Uses talk to organise sequence and clarify thinking, ideas, feelings and events. **CLL Linking sounds and letters 3:** Use their phonic knowledge to write simple regular words and make phonetically plausible attempts at more complex words. **CLL Writing 3:** Write their own names and other things such as labels and captions, and begin to form simple sentences, sometimes using punctuation. **CLL Writing 2:** Attempt writing for different purposes, using features of different forms such as lists, stories and instructions.
5	Write	**CLL Writing 5:** Use their phonic knowledge to write simple regular words and make phonetically plausible attempts at more complex words. **CLL Writing 3:** Write their own names and other things such as labels and captions, and begin to form simple sentences, sometimes using punctuation. **CLL Language for thinking 5:** Use talk to organise, sequence and clarify thinking, ideas, feelings and events. **CLL Language for communication 12:** Speak clearly and audibly with confidence and control and show awareness of the listener. **CLL Language for communication 14:** Have confidence to speak to others about wants and interests.
6	Extended Writing	**CLL Language for thinking 5:** Uses talk to organise sequence and clarify thinking, ideas, feelings and events. **CLL Writing 2:** Attempt writing for different purposes, using features of different forms such as lists, stories and instructions. **CLL Writing 5:** Use their phonic knowledge to write simple regular words and make phonetically plausible attempts at more complex words.

Unit	*Stories for Writing*	Scottish Curriculum for Excellence objectives
1	Talk Read	**LIT 0-04a** I listen or watch for useful or interesting information and I use this to make choices or learn new things. **LIT 0-11b** I enjoy exploring and choosing stories and other texts to watch, read or listen to and can share my likes and dislikes. **LIT 0-07a** To help me understand stories and other texts , I ask questions and link what I am learning with what I already know. **ENG 0-12a** I explore sounds, letters and words, discovering how they work together, and I can use what I learn to help me as I read and write. **LIT 0-01c, LIT 0-19a** I enjoy exploring events and characters in stories and other texts, sharing my thoughts in different ways.
2	Read Tell	**LIT 0-01c** I enjoy exploring events and characters in stories and other texts, sharing my thoughts in different ways. **LIT 0-09b** I enjoy exploring events and characters in stories and other texts, and I use what I learn to invent my own, sharing them with others. **LIT 0-09a** Within real and imaginary situations, I share experiences and feelings, ideas and information in a way that communicates my message. **LIT 0-10a** As I listen and take part in conversations and discussions, I discover new words and phrases which I use to help me express my ideas thoughts and feelings. **LIT 0-07a** To help me understand stories and other texts, I ask questions and link what I am learning with what I already know.
3	Tell Write	**LIT 0-01c** I enjoy exploring events and characters in stories and other texts, sharing my thoughts in different ways. **LIT 0-01a** I enjoy exploring and playing with the patterns and sounds of language, and can use what I learn. **ENG 0-31a** I enjoy exploring events and characters in stories and other texts and I use what I learn to invent my own, sharing these with others in imaginative ways. **LIT 0-20a** I enjoy exploring and playing with the patterns and sounds of language and can use what I learn. **LIT 0-02a** As I listen and talk in different situations, I am learning to take turns and am developing my awareness of when to talk and when to listen.
4	Write	**LIT 0-09b, LIT 0-31a** I enjoy exploring events and characters in stories and other texts and I use what I learn to invent my own, sharing these with others in imaginative ways. **LIT 0-21b** As I play and learn, I enjoy exploring interesting materials for writing and different ways of recording my experiences and feelings, ideas and information. **LIT 0-20a** I enjoy exploring and playing with the patterns and sounds of language and can use what I learn. **LIT 0-21a** I explore sounds, letters and words, discovering how they work together, and I can use what I learn to help me as I read or write.
5	Write	**LIT 0-21a** I explore sounds, letters and words, discovering how they work together, and I can use what I learn to help me as I read and write. **LIT 0-20a** I enjoy exploring and playing with the patterns and sounds of language and can use what I learn. **LIT 0-07a** To help me understand stories and other texts, I ask questions and link what I am learning with what I already know. **ENG 0-21b** As I play and learn, I enjoy exploring interesting materials for writing and different ways of recording my experiences and feelings, ideas and information. **ENG 0-31a** I enjoy exploring events and characters in stories and other texts and I use what I learn to invent my own, sharing these with others in imaginative ways.
6	Extended Writing	**LIT 0-26a** Within real and imaginary situations, I share experiences and feelings, ideas and information in a way that communicates my message. **ENG 0-31a** I enjoy exploring events and characters in stories… and I use what I learn to invent my own, sharing these with others in imaginative ways. **LIT 0-21b** As I play and learn, I enjoy exploring interesting materials for writing and different ways of recording my experiences and feelings, ideas and information. **LIT 0-21a** I explore sounds, letters and words, discovering how they work together, and I can use what I learn to help me as I read or write.

Objectives Chart for *My Brother*

This chart shows the Early Years Foundation Stage and Scottish Curriculum for Excellence objectives that can be covered using the teaching notes for *My Brother* (pages 42 to 49) and the detailed planning grids on the Planning CD-ROM. The Planning CD-ROM shows how the teaching breaks down into six units of work, with five sessions in each unit.

Unit	*Stories for Writing*	Early Years Foundation Stage objectives
1	Talk Read	**CLL Language for communication 14:** Have confidence to speak to others about their own wants and interests. **CLL Language for communication 7:** Sustain attentive listening, responding to what they have heard with relevant comments, questions or actions. **CLL Language for thinking 5:** Use talk to organize, sequence and clarify thinking, ideas, feelings and events. **CLL Reading 1:** Show an understanding of the elements of stories, such as main character, sequence of events and openings. **CLL Language for communication 15:** Extend their vocabulary, exploring the meanings and sounds of new words.
2	Read Tell	**CLL Language for thinking 2:** Use language to imagine and recreate roles and experiences. **CLL Reading 1:** Show an understanding of the elements of stories, such as main character, sequence of events and openings. **CLL Reading 3:** Re-tell narratives in the correct sequence, drawing on language patterns of stories. **CLL Language for thinking 5:** Use talk to organise, sequence and clarify thinking, ideas, feelings and events.
3	Tell Write	**CLL Language for communication 10:** Listen with enjoyment, and respond to stories, songs, rhymes and poems, and make up their own. **CLL Reading 3:** Re-tell narratives in the correct sequence, drawing on language patterns of stories. **CLL Writing 2:** Attempt writing for different purposes, using features of different forms such as lists, stories and instructions. **CLL Writing 5:** Use their phonic knowledge to write simple regular words and make phonetically plausible attempts at more complex words.
4	Write	**CLL Language for thinking 2:** Use language to imagine and recreate roles and experiences. **CLL Writing 2:** Attempt writing for different purposes, using features of different forms such as lists, stories and instructions. **CLL Writing 3:** Write their own names and other things such as labels and captions, and begin to form simple sentences, sometimes using punctuation. **CLL Writing 7:** Use phonic knowledge to write simple regular words and make phonetically plausible attempts at more complex words.
5	Write	**CLL Language for communication 6:** Interact with others, negotiating plans and activities and taking turns in conversation. **CLL Writing 5:** Use phonic knowledge to write simple regular words and make phonetically plausible attempts at more complex words. **CLL Language for communication 12:** Speak clearly and audibly with confidence and control and show awareness of the listener. **CLL Language for communication 7:** Sustain attentive listening, responding to what they have heard with relevant comments, questions or actions.
6	Extended Writing	**CLL Language for communication 6:** Interact with others, negotiating plans and activities and taking turns in conversation. **CLL Writing 5:** Use phonic knowledge to write simple regular words and make phonetically plausible attempts at more complex words. **CLL Writing 2:** Attempt writing for different purposes, using features of different forms such as lists, stories and instructions. **CLL Language for thinking 5:** Use talk to organize, sequence and clarify thinking, ideas, feelings and events.

Unit	*Stories for Writing*	Scottish Curriculum for Excellence objectives
1	Talk Read	**LIT 0-02a** As I listen and talk in different situations, I am learning to take turns and am developing my awareness of when to talk and when to listen. **LIT 0-11b** I enjoy exploring and choosing stories and other texts to watch, read and listen to, and can share my likes and dislikes. **ENG 0-12a** I explore sounds, letters and words, discovering how they work together, and I can use what I learn to help me as I read and write. **LIT 0-19a** I enjoy exploring events and characters in stories and other texts, sharing my thoughts in different ways.
2	Read Tell	**LIT 0-01c** I enjoy exploring events and characters in stories and other texts, sharing my thoughts in different ways. **LIT 0-31a** I enjoy exploring events and characters in stories and other texts, and I use what I learn to invent my own, sharing these with others in imaginative ways. **LIT 0-09a** Within real and imaginary situations, I share experiences and feelings, ideas and information in away that communicate my message. **LIT 0-07a** To help me understand stories and other texts, I ask questions and link what I am learning with what I already know
3	Tell Write	**LIT 0-01c** I enjoy exploring events and characters in stories and other texts, sharing my thoughts in different ways. **LIT 0-09a** Within real and imaginary situations, I share experiences and feelings, ideas and information in a way that communicate my message. **LIT 0-31a** I enjoy exploring events and characters in stories and other texts and I use what I learn to invent my own, sharing these with others in imaginative ways. **LIT 0-20a** I enjoy exploring and playing with the patterns and sounds of language and can use what I learn. **LIT 0-07a** To help me understand stories and other texts, I ask questions and link what I am learning to what I already know.
4	Write	**LIT 0-26a** Within real and imaginary situations, I share experiences and feelings, ideas and information in a way that communicates my message. **LIT 0-07a** To help me understand stories and other texts, I ask questions and link what I am learning with what I already know. **LIT 0-20a** I enjoy exploring and playing with the patterns and sounds of language and can use what I learn. **LIT 0-21a** I explore sounds, letters and words, discovering how they work together, and I can use what I learn to help me as I read or write.
5	Write	**LIT 0-21a, ENG 0-12a** I explore sounds, letters and words, discovering how they work together, and I can use what I learn to help me as I read and write. **ENG 0-31a** I enjoy exploring events and characters in stories and other texts, and I use what I learn to invent my own, sharing these with others in imaginative ways. **LIT 0-09a** I enjoy exploring events and characters in stories and other texts and I use what I learn to invent my own, sharing these with others in imaginative ways. **LIT 0-14a** I use signs, books or other texts to find useful or interesting information and I use this to plan, make choices or learn new things.
6	Extended Writing	**LIT 0-02a** As I listen and talk in different situations, I am learning to take turns and am developing my awareness of when to talk and when to listen. **LIT 0-19a** I enjoy exploring events and characters in stories and other texts, sharing my thoughts in different ways. **LIT 0-21b** As I play and learn, I enjoy exploring interesting materials for writing and different ways of recording my experiences and feelings, ideas and information. **LIT 0-07a** To help me understand stories and other texts, I ask questions and link what I am learning with what I already know. **LIT 0-31a** I enjoy exploring events and characters in stories and other texts and I use what I learn to invent my own, sharing these with others in imaginative ways.

How to use the CD-ROM

MAIN MENU

You can access all areas of the CD content through the Main menu

Select a book to get started

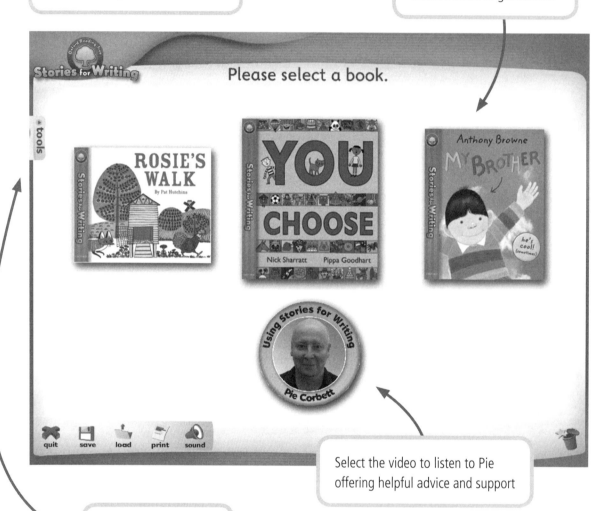

Select the video to listen to Pie offering helpful advice and support

Fully interact with the stories and story maps using the toolbar

BOOK MENU

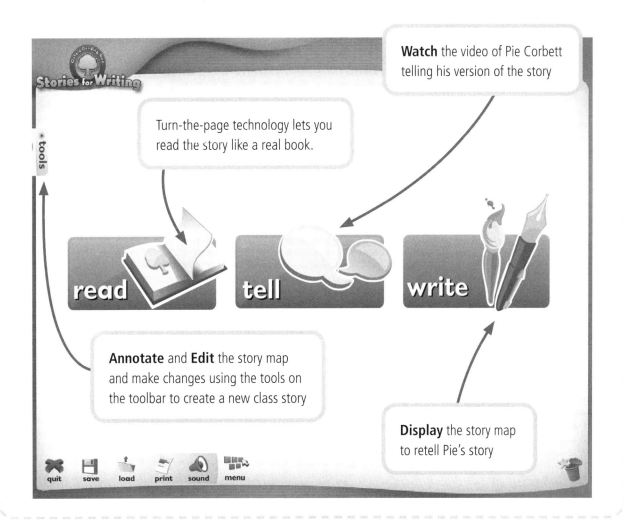

Watch the video of Pie Corbett telling his version of the story

Turn-the-page technology lets you read the story like a real book.

Annotate and **Edit** the story map and make changes using the tools on the toolbar to create a new class story

Display the story map to retell Pie's story

read   tell   write

quit   save   load   print   sound   menu

HOW TO USE THE TOOLS

Fully interact with the picture books on screen by using the toolbar.

 Drag the **speech** and **thought bubbles** and **sticky notes** to type in text that shows what a character might be saying or thinking or to annotate the text.

 Use the **zoom** tool to enlarge the illustrations so you can see more details. Depending on your whiteboard, select the page with your whiteboard stylus or finger to zoom around the page.

 Use the **highlighter** tool to identify words, phrases, sentences or punctuation in the story.

 Use the **grab** tool to move annotations on the screen.

 Use the **pen tool** to annotate the story text, write replacement synonyms, collect the children's ideas and make changes to Pie's story map.

 If you have the tool bar open and you are using an annotation tool, select the **control** tool to return to the story controls.

How to use the picture books

AT SCHOOL

The *Stories for Writing* storybooks have been chosen because they are favourite children's books with enormous potential for talking and writing. They are not books that all children could be expected to read independently, so the notes on the inside back covers of the books will help you to support children in group and guided reading sessions.

Knowing the book deeply

Pie Corbett suggests that we loiter with stories, getting to know them really well. The activities in the Read and Tell sections of *Stories for Writing* give ample opportunities to do just this. Use the question prompts, activities, role-play and drama to explore the book at many levels. Make a role-play area in your classroom and use the cross-curricular ideas so that children can engage with the story at every opportunity. The extended writing activities can be used at any point you feel appropriate.

Read together on screen

Play the storybook on screen so that the children listen to the story being read to them. You can use the story to model reading strategies and highlight words to reinforce phonic skills or strategies to remember tricky high frequency words.

Reading is not just the process of decoding and by using the storybook on screen you will discover a rich resource for reading as a writer as well as inferential and deductive questioning, which are all supported in the notes in this handbook.

Read together as a group

The notes on the inside back covers of the storybooks give guidance for group or guided reading sessions in class.

AT HOME

Children can take the special educational editions of the storybooks home with them to share what they know about the story with their parents and carers, as well as to enjoy reading the story with them.

The notes on the inside front covers give parents and carers ideas for reading and exploring the storybook with their child. Children are not expected to be able to read the book independently but rather to enjoy retelling the story, talking about the pictures, characters and events, and spending time doing the suggested activities together.

Why Pie chose the picture books

ROSIE'S WALK

- *Rosie's Walk* is one of my favourite stories and children love it!

- The illustrations are funny and share a clever joke with young readers.

- This is a circular story – the story ends where it begins. This is great for early storytelling and writing.

- Rosie and the fox are archetypal characters (goodie and baddie). This helps children to imagine their own characters when writing.

Rosie the hen went for a walk

- So much isn't said about the characters, which provides lots of creative opportunities for talking and writing.

YOU CHOOSE

- When my children were younger we used to spend hours reading books where they could choose what they liked.

- *You Choose* has endless possibilities and asks the reader to make lots of choices.

- *You Choose* gives children a bank of settings, characters and props from all the different story genres.

- *You Choose* asks questions and encourages children to frame their own.

MY BROTHER

- I love this book because I have got four brothers!

- *My Brother* is full of clever visual jokes and vivid illustrations which tickle and entice anyone who reads the book.

- I like the way it creates a happy, lively picture of childhood.

- Like Anthony Browne, I think it is important to concentrate on the good things about the people we know and love.

- The language is very direct and appealing and is a great model for children's own writing.

About the storybook authors and illustrators

ROSIE'S WALK

Pat Hutchins was born in Yorkshire, the second youngest of a large family.

- At sixteen she won a scholarship to Darlington Art School.
- She wrote and illustrated *Rosie's Walk* in 1968 and it has been a classic ever since.
- Other books by Pat Hutchins include: *Happy Birthday Sam, The House that Sailed Away, Don't forget the bacon!, The Wind Blew, Titch* and *Follow that Bus.*

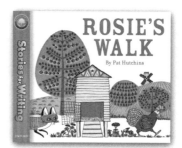

YOU CHOOSE

Pippa Goodhart was born in Granchester, Leicester in 1958.

- Her cat once stole the next door neighbour's Christmas lunch!
- Her mum helped her to learn to read by making up stories and she still remembers one called *Hickey Honkers.*
- She worked for five years in a bookshop before becoming an author.
- Her favourite book is *Dogger* by Shirley Hughes.

Nick Sharratt was born in London in 1962.

- He sold his first picture for five pounds when he was 9 years old!
- He has illustrated over 40 books.
- He was the official World Book Day illustrator in 2006.
- He keeps a shop dummy in his studio and has been to evening classes in juggling!

MY BROTHER

Anthony Browne became The Children's Laureate in 2009.

- He grew up in a pub in Yorkshire and wanted to be a cartoonist or boxer when he grew up.

- His favourite children's illustrator is Maurice Sendak who wrote *Where the Wild Things are.*

- Children in a primary school, inspired by the books *My Mum* and *My Dad* by Anthony Browne, wrote their own book called *My Brother.* When Anthony Browne visited them he was so inspired by their idea that he wrote this book!

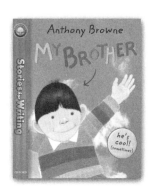

Rosie's Walk

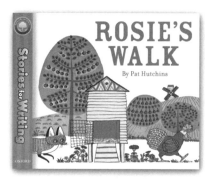

TALK

- Before reading the book, talk about the countryside and what animals you might find there.
- Talk about which animals are wild and which animals we farm.
- Ask the children what we get from the animals we farm.

 Use Resource Sheet 1 on page 50 to sort wild and farm animals.

READ

1 Read the story together

- Select *Rosie's Walk* on the CD-ROM.
- Click on *Read* to listen to the story being read from beginning to end without interruption.

- Enjoy the story and let the children discuss any aspect they are interested in.
- Let the children raise their own questions.

2 Book Talk

- Reread the story and make sure it is on display whilst you explore these open questions. Make this session exciting and dynamic by encouraging paired and group discussions and interact with the text using the zoom, sticky notes and annotating tools to record the children's responses and ideas.

  o *Can you say what the book was about?*
  o *Which picture do you think is the funniest?*
  o *Tell me about why the fox is following Rosie.*
  o *What would you say to Rosie if you could talk to her?*
  o *Do you think Rosie knew the fox was following her?*

- Talk about the pictures.
- Stop at points in the book and ask:

  o *What do you think is happening in this picture?*
  o *Tell me about what Rosie might be thinking.*
  o *What do you think the fox is going to do next?*
  o *How do you think the fox is feeling here?*

 Use Resource Sheet 2 on page 51 for children to note a personal response to the story.

 **READ**

3 Explore the story

Setting: farmyard in the countryside

- Display the title page showing the farmyard.

- Ask the children to pretend they are in the farmyard so they can talk about what they can see or hear.

- Ask the children to imagine they are in Rosie's farmyard. Ask them to think of words and phrases to describe the farmyard setting. Use the sticky notes tool to record these on the page.

Characters: Rosie and the fox

- Ask children to think of words to describe what Rosie is like and write them on labels (for example, *small*, *crafty*, *clever*, *cunning*, *funny*, *lucky*, *hungry*).

- Ask children to think of words to describe what the fox is like and write them on labels (for example, *funny*, *big*, *silly*, *clumsy*, *crafty*, *unlucky*, *hungry*, *hunter*).

- Display a big picture of Rosie and a big picture of the fox on the classroom wall. Label the pictures with the children's descriptive words.

Word and Language Games: prepositions

- Read the book together again. *Which words tell us where Rosie is going?* Use the highlighter tool to highlight the prepositional language (*across*, *around*, *over*, *past*, *through*, *under*).

- Use simple actions to mirror the words as you read them. For example, sweep your hand in a circle as you read the word *around*.

- **Game: Farmyard animals.** Set up a small world farmyard with a group of children. Direct the children to move the animals around the farmyard using prepositional language (*up*, *over*, *under*, *through*, etc).

Role-play and Drama

- Ask the children to get into pairs and hot seat one another, answering questions in role as the hen and then the fox.

- In role, pretend to be the farmer and get children to ask you questions about Rosie the hen and your farm.

 Use Resource Sheet 3 and Resource Sheet 4 on pages 52–53 to create hen and fox masks for role-play activities.

4 Guided/group and independent reading

Rosie the hen went for a walk

- You will find ideas for parents/carers to use when reading *Rosie's Walk* with their child at home on the inside front cover of the storybook.

- You will find ideas for using *Rosie's Walk* for guided/group reading on the inside back cover of the storybook.

An extract from *Rosie's Walk*, by Pat Hutchins, with kind permission from Random House Children's Books

READ

5 Reading as a Writer

Return to the book and use it to explore the questions below, beginning to think about what might be needed to create your own version.

Plot

- Discuss with the children the kind of story *Rosie's Walk* is. It is a journey story, which is circular. It starts and ends in the same place.

- Discuss how the fox follows Rosie.

Setting

- *Where is Rosie's Walk set?* A farmyard, in the countryside.

- *Where else could Rosie's Walk be set?* In a city farm, in a back garden, in a field, etc.

- *Where else might Rosie go for a walk?* She could walk: along the river bank, around the field, to the next farm, etc.

- *Which different places might Rosie visit on the way?* She could visit: an orchard, another animal, a barn, the milking shed etc.

Character

- How many main characters are there in *Rosie's Walk*? There are two main characters – Rosie and the fox.

- Talk about how one character is clever and one character gets fooled.

Language

- Reread the story. *Are there any other words that we could use to describe where Rosie is going?* (For example, *along, by, up, on, down, out, into* etc.)

6 Other stories to read

Journey stories

- *Little Red Hen*
- *Chicken Licken*
- *We're Going on a Bear Hunt* by Michael Rosen

Stories written by Pat Hutchins

- The *Titch* stories
- *Happy Birthday Sam*
- *The House that Sailed Away*
- *The Wind Blew*
- *Follow that Bus*
- *We're Going on a Picnic*

7 Links to Oxford Reading Tree classic stories Stages 1–2

- Spot *Rosie's Walk* on a bookshelf in: *The Library* (Stage 1)

- Left to right directionality: *Fetch!* (Stage 1)

- Prepositional language: *Look Out!* (Stage 1) and *Up and Down* (Stage 2)

- Sharing books: *Six in a Bed* (Stage 1)

- Journeys: *The Lost Teddy* (Stage 1), *Push!* (Stage 1+), *Fun at the Beach* (Stage 1), *The Journey* (Stage 1)

- Animal chases: *Go Away, Cat!* (Stage 1+) and *The Chase* (Stage 2)

- Creatures in the wild: *The Hedgehog* (Stage 1), and *What Is It?* (Stage 2)

ROSIE'S WALK

TELL

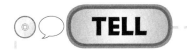

1 Imitate: *Rosie's Walk*

- The children need to fully understand and internalise the story before they move on to telling Pie's simple innovated story.
- Keep reading and joining in with the story until they know it word for word.
- Emphasise the prepositional language as you retell the story, to highlight where Rosie is going on her walk.
- To help them remember the story, act it out.
- If appropriate, use an enlarged copy of the *Rosie's Walk* story map on Resource Sheet 5 for children to retell the story in their own words, or draw your own.

Use Resource Sheet 5 on page 54 to retell *Rosie's Walk* as a class.

2 Simple patterned innovation: Pie Corbett's story

- Tell the class that they are going to learn how to tell a new story, *Gordon's Walk.* It is similar to *Rosie's Walk,* but some things have changed.
- At this level, the simple patterned language of the sentences makes the story structure very predictable. Only very simple changes are made, such as names, places and verbs, which slot perfectly into the original sentence structure.
- Click on *Tell* to play the video of Pie Corbett telling the story of *Gordon's Walk* using his story map and actions. Encourage the class to join in.
- Replay the video many times. As the children become more confident, gradually turn down the volume so that they retell the story without Pie's voice.
- Ask the children to retell the story as a class, then in groups or pairs, before they have a go on their own.
- Retelling is not a memory game. Most children will need to see a story map, do the actions and possibly use objects, to retell the story clearly.
- An enlarged photocopy of the story map, or your own version of it, should always be displayed.

Use Resource Sheet 6 on page 55 for children to use to retell *Gordon's Walk.* Some children may want to create their own story maps. Resource Sheet 7 on page 56 shows Pie's story script.

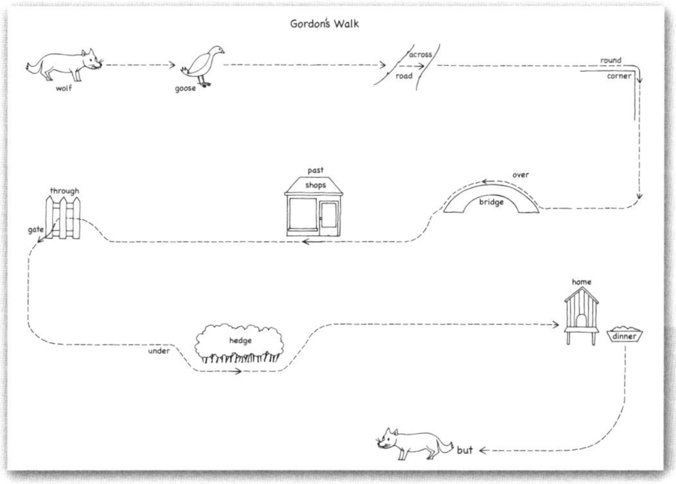

A story map of Pie's simple innovated story, *Gordon's Walk*

WRITE

1 Planning together

- Click on *Write* to use Pie's story map to help you create a shared, simple innovated class story.

- Make simple changes and practise each one as you add them to the story map on screen or on a flip chart. In this way your own version of the story will gradually develop.

- Ensure the children are involved in this process, using partner talk to make up their ideas.

- Ideas for changes include:

  - Change the characters, e.g. a duck and a cat or a rabbit and a wolf.

  - Decide on the journey, e.g. around the field, into the farmer's garden, along the riverbank.

  - Change the names, e.g. Dan the duck or Kit the cat.

  - Add adjectives, e.g. old farmyard, deep pond, tall haycock.

2 Shared writing

- As well as simple changes, try adding in extra details to embellish the story. This could be 'dropping in' words (adjectives) or adding whole sentences and chunks of text.

- Once the children know the new class story, move into shared writing.

  - Focus on the sequence of the story and ask them to tell their partner where they think the character is going next.

  - Help the children remember the order by using time connectives to order the story (first, next, then, after that, finally) with actions.

  - Tell the children to use their story maps and actions to retell the story in the right order.

3 Recording children creating their own stories

- Lead children through developing their own map based on this story.

- In pairs, encourage them to tell and retell their version before recording it.

- Work with groups, pairs or individual children to help them record stories at their own level.

Children can:

- dictate to an adult who scribes
- record their story using a microphone
- video their story with a digital camera
- perform to a group
- create their own mark-making
- attempt writing.

ROSIE'S WALK

WRITE

4 Guided writing

Focus: retell narratives in the correct sequence drawing on language patterns of stories (EYF CCL Reading scale point 7)

- Display the shared, simple innovated class story map.
- Ask the children to identify all the different places the main characters visit on their walk.
- Use small world figures to act out the story. Encourage the children to join in to embed the patterned language and actions for the prepositions.
- Ask the children to work in pairs, telling the story to each other.

- You can differentiate this session for less confident and more confident children.

  - Work as a group to sequence and compose the story, which you scribe as a group text.
  - Challenge the children to try to sequence the story independently, writing captions if appropriate.

5 Assessing children's writing

Focus: retell narratives in the correct sequence drawing on language patterns of stories (EYF CCL Reading scale point 7)

- Focus on the children's control of the story narrative. Confident storytellers will use the patterned language to allow them to do more than just repeat the story. Can they use the story map, intonation and gestures to tell more than just the basic story plot? For some children, a direct retelling of the narrative is enough of a challenge. Less confident children should be encouraged to retell the story in a small group.
- Record children's ability and confidence in retelling a simple tale.

- All children can improve their story retelling by:

  - Drawing a story map or a story board before writing.
  - Telling their story to a partner before writing to check that it flows.
  - Having visual prompts to help them during their retelling.
  - Drawing their own story map so they have ownership of the story.
  - Doing actions as they retell the story.
  - Having lots of practice in short bursts to build their confidence.

EXTENDED WRITING

1 A 'Wanted' poster for the fox

- Tell the children that the farmer has found out about the fox and wants their help in making a 'Wanted' poster.

- Re-visit the words that they used to describe the fox and work together to orally compose sentences to describe it.

- Talk about what the fox has done wrong and work together to compose a sentence.

- Photocopy your scribed 'Wanted' poster for the children to add to and draw the fox on.

 Use Resource Sheet 8 on page 57 to create a 'Wanted' poster.

2 Farm environmental print

- Remind the children about the words on the corn and flour sacks in *Rosie's Walk*.

- Show them some images of a farm and talk about the signs, symbols and labelling.

- Work together to make a sign for a farm to use in the role-play area.

3 Information about chickens

- Show the children some examples of information texts about chickens. Explain that these types of books tell us facts about things like animals.

- Discuss chickens, collecting children's ideas to use later. (For example, they scratch in the dirt, they have feathers, they eat corn, etc.)

- Work together to write labels in the callouts on Resource Sheet 9. Orally compose a sentence for each heading and then scribe it for the group.

 Use Resource Sheet 9 on page 58 to collect information about chickens in a writing frame.

4 Tickets for entry to a family farm

- Show the children some examples of tickets from outings or trips. Explain that a ticket gives you information.

- Talk about what information you may need on a ticket and use Resource Sheet 10 to scribe a ticket for entry to a family farm.

- Use the tickets in the role-play area.

 Use Resource Sheet 10 on page 59 to complete a template of a ticket.

5 Big Book

- Make a class big book version of the new class story including children's illustrations.

CROSS-CURRICULAR ACTIVITIES

Creating Dance and Music

- Create sounds for all the animals in the story using percussion instruments.
- Sing *Old MacDonald had a Farm* and *Five Little Ducks went Swimming one day.*

Exploring Media and Materials

- Talk about the stylized artwork, which uses repeated patterns and prints.
- Create repeated patterns using, for example, leaves, cut-up fruit, feathers, potato prints.

Knowledge and Understanding of the World

Design and making:
- Look at the different mini-beasts in the story such as butterflies, bees, grasshoppers, spiders, wasps, snails.
- Make a mini-beast mobile. Get the children to cut out or decorate pictures of mini-beasts. Connect them together to make a mobile using straws, string and sticky tape.

Place:
- Go on a journey to a local shop or around the school.
- Make a map of the journey using pictures, symbols and/or words.

Exploration and investigation:
- The farm in *Rosie's Walk* has a flourmill.
- Find out about what you can make with flour and explore how cooking with flour makes food (e.g. cakes, bread, pizza, pasta, etc).
- Choose a recipe using flour and make it with small groups of children.

Problem Solving, Reasoning and Numeracy

Shape, space and measures:
- Talk about the different buildings in the book and name the shapes that they are made of.
- Cut out different shapes to make some of the farm buildings.

Physical development

Movement and space:
- Use the prepositional language from the story (across, around, over, past, through, under) as instructions for the children to move around objects either in the hall or outside.

Personal Social and Emotional Development

Behaviour and self-control:
- Talk about who is doing the right thing in the story.
- What are the consequences of Rosie's actions and the fox's actions?
- Do the children think that what happens to the fox is fair?

Role-play area

- Create a farmyard or simple floor 'map' which can be used with small animal toys for storytelling.
- Children work in pairs to perform their own version of the story.

> **Check out the *Stories for Writing* Planning CD-ROM for week-by-week literacy plans, exciting cross-curricular ideas and extra resource sheets.**

You Choose

TALK

- Before reading the book, talk about the choices the children made this morning.

- *What did they have for breakfast? What did they choose to bring to school? What book did they choose to read this morning?*

Use Resource Sheet 1 on page 60 for the children to draw their choices.

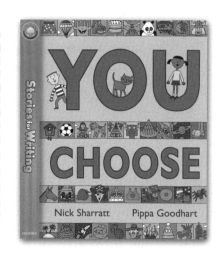

Nick Sharratt   Pippa Goodhart

READ

1 Read the story together

- Select *You Choose* on the CD-ROM.

- Click on *Read* to listen to the story being read from beginning to end without interruption.

- Enjoy the story and let the children discuss any aspect they are interested in.

- Let the children raise their own questions.

2 Book Talk

- Reread the book and make sure it is on display whilst you explore these open questions. Make this session exciting and dynamic by encouraging paired and group discussions and interact with the text using the zoom, sticky notes and annotating tools to record the children's responses and ideas.

  - *What sort of book is this?*
  - *Is there anything you wouldn't like to choose?*
  - *Which is the silliest choice?*
  - *Why do you think the author chose to start with 'Where would you go?' and end with 'Where would you sleep?'*

- Talk about the pictures.

- Stop at points in the book and ask:

  - *What do you think is happening in this picture?*
  - *Tell me five words to describe this character/ creature.*
  - *What would you do here?*
  - *What do you think about the character's choice on this page?*
  - *What do you think a princess/ogre/elf/your friend would choose on this page?*

Use Resource Sheet 2 on page 61 for children to note a personal response to the story.

3 Explore the story

Setting: If you could go anywhere...

- Display the pages with the question *'If you could go anywhere'* and ask: *Which looks the best place for an adventure?* Encourage the children to give reasons for their choices.

- Use the zoom tool to look at details like the shooting star and rocket ship and ask the children to think of words to describe what they can see.

- Ask: *Which place is the most secret/ noisiest/exciting/scary/fun?* Encourage the children to come up and talk about the setting they would choose and explain why.

Characters: family and friends

- Display the pages with the question *'Who would you like for your family and friends?'* Ask: *I wonder what these characters would say if they could talk to us?*

- Click on the speech bubble in the toolbar and scribe the children's suggestions for the different characters.

- Ask the children to say which characters are from storybooks and talk about the books you might find them in.

> Use Resource Sheet 3 on page 62 to choose four storybook characters for a 'Great Characters for Stories' display.

Word and Language Games: descriptions

- Display the pages with the question *'And what would you put in it?'* Ask: *What do you think could be behind the secret door?*

- Ask the children to have a go at describing something on the page to the class without saying its name; the other children should guess what they are describing.

- **Game: Secret Door!** Make your own secret door for a class display and ask children to draw or cut out pictures to stick behind it. Describe what is behind the door and see if the children can guess what is behind it each day.

> Use Resource Sheet 4 on page 63 for the children to draw what could be behind the secret door.

Role-play and Drama

- Display the page with the question *' … or perhaps a hat?'* and talk about the different hats. Ask: *What characters do the different hats remind you of? Tell me more about...* (pointing to one of the characters). *What might they say?*

- Ask the children to put on imaginary hats and act in role. Can the class guess what hat the child has put on?

4 Guided/group and independent reading

- You will find ideas for parents/carers to use when reading *You Choose* with their child at home on the inside front cover of the storybook.

- You will find ideas for using *You Choose* for guided/group reading on the inside back cover of the storybook.

An extract from *You Choose*, by Pippa Goodhart and Nick Sharratt, with kind permission from Random House Children's Books

5 Reading as a Writer

Return to the book and use it to explore the questions below, beginning to think about what might be needed to create your own version.

Plot

- Discuss with children the kind of book *You Choose* is. It asks questions and lists things that you'd like to choose.
- *Which other things could you choose?* (For example, trips out, ice-cream flavours, toys.) Collect a list of other ideas for a new page in the book.

Setting

- *Where else could you choose to go?*
- Use holiday brochures, maps and magazines to create a collage of different settings, for example the jungle, the Arctic, a desert island, etc.

Character

- How many main characters are there in *You Choose?* There are three – the cat, the girl and the boy.
- Look through the book and think about the choices other characters might make.

Language

- Reread the story. *Are there any words that ask questions?* (For example, *if, where, who, what, would, when*, etc.)
- *What other words could we use to ask questions?* (For example, *can, how, could, why, which*, etc.)
- Compose new questions for *You Choose*.

6 Other stories to read

Choosing and list stories

- ○ *Goldilocks and the Three Bears*
- ○ *Little Red Riding Hood*
- ○ *The Three Little Pigs*
- ○ *Cinderella*
- ○ *Eat Your Peas* by Nick Sharratt

Stories written by Pippa Goodhart

- ○ *Eat Your Peas* and other *Daisy* books
- ○ *Octopus Socktopus*
- ○ *Shark in the Dark*

Stories by Nick Sharratt

- ○ *Slow Magic*
- ○ *Pam's Maps*
- ○ *Eat Your Peas*

7 Links to Oxford Reading Tree classic stories Stages 1–2

- Question words: *Is It?* (Stage 1), *Can You See Me?* (Stage 1+), *What Is It?* (Stage 2)
- Places: *At School* (Stage 1), *Fun at the Beach* (Stage 1), *The Haircut* (Stage 1), *The Library* (Stage 1), *The Pet Shop* (Stage 2)
- Likes and Dislikes: *What a Din!* (Stage 1+), *Top Dog* (Stage 1+), *What Dogs Like* (Stage 1+), *Look After Me* (Stage 1+)
- Choices: *What a Bad Dog!* (Stage 2), *The Go-Kart* (Stage 2)

YOU CHOOSE

TELL

1 Imitate: *You Choose*

- The children need to fully understand and internalise the book before they move on to telling Pie's simple innovated version.

- Try to embed some of the key phrases and patterned language so the children are familiar with the structures in the book.

- Emphasise the question words as you retell *You Choose*, to highlight what sorts of decisions the reader is being asked to make.

- Keep reading and joining in with the story until the children know it well.

- If appropriate, use an enlarged copy of the *You Choose* story map on Resource Sheet 5 for children to retell the story in their own words, or draw your own.

 Use Resource Sheet 5 on page 64 to retell *You Choose* as a class.

2 Simple patterned innovation: Pie Corbett's story

- Tell the class that they are going to learn how to tell a new version of *You Choose.* It is similar to the original version, but some things have changed.

- At this level, the simple patterned language of the sentences makes the structure very predictable. Only very simple changes are made.

- Click on *Tell* to play the video of Pie Corbett telling his version of *You Choose* using his story map and actions. Encourage the class to join in.

- Replay the video a number of times. As the children become more confident, gradually turn down the volume so that they retell the innovated version without Pie's voice.

- Ask the children to retell this version as a class, then in groups or pairs, before they have a go on their own.

- Retelling is not a memory game. Most children will need to see a story map, do the actions and possibly use objects, to retell *You Choose* clearly.

- An enlarged photocopy of the story map, or your own version of it, should always be displayed.

 Use Resource Sheet 6 on page 65 for children to use to retell *You Choose*. Some children may want to create their own story maps. Resource Sheet 7 on page 66 shows Pie's script.

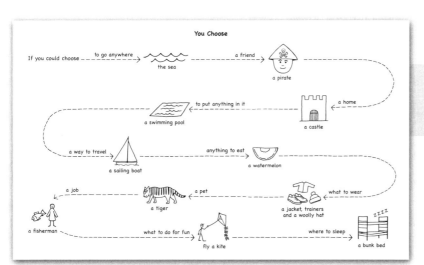

A story map of Pie's simple innovated version of *You Choose*

WRITE

1 Planning together

- Click on *Write* to use Pie's story map to help you create a shared, simple innovated class version.

- Make similar changes and practise each one as you add them to the story map on screen or on a flip chart. In this way, your own version of the story will gradually develop.

- Ensure the children are involved in this process, using partner talk to make up their ideas.

- Ideas to get started include:

  o Using the same pattern as the one that Pie based his version on.

  o Making simple changes and choices.

2 Shared writing

- As well as simple changes, try adding in extra details to embellish the story. This could be 'dropping in' words (adjectives) or adding whole sentences and chunks of text.

- Once the children know the new class story, move into shared writing.

  o Develop a simple pattern.

  o Involve the children in making choices and changes.

  o Use the story map to help write the new version and turn it into a big book.

3 Recording children creating their own stories

- Lead children through developing their own map based on this story.

- In pairs, encourage them to tell and retell their version before recording it.

- Work with groups, pairs or individual children to help them record stories at their own level.

Children can:

o dictate to an adult who scribes

o record their version using a microphone

o video their version with a digital camera

o perform to a group

o create their own mark-making

o attempt writing.

WRITE

4 Guided writing

Focus: attempt writing for a variety of purposes using features of different forms (EYF CCL Writing scale point 6)

- This session should occur once the children have composed some of their own version (orally, scribed or written).

- Write the beginning of the sentence *Where would you like to...* and collect ideas on how the question could finish. Scribe an ending, highlighting the question mark.

- Invite the children to use the same pattern and a different question word to start another question. Model writing this for the children.

- Repeat this for each of the question words. Make sure the children can see these question starts as they write their own question/s.

- You can differentiate this session for less confident and more confident children.

> o **Work as a group to compose questions and answer them orally.**
>
> o **Challenge children to frame their own questions.**

5 Assessing children's writing

Focus: attempt writing for a variety of purposes using features of different forms (EYF CCL Writing scale point 6)

- Focus on the children's choice of question starts. Are they appropriate for the question? Does the question make sense? Confident children will be able to frame their questions using question words adapted to the context.

- Record children's ability and confidence in drawing and retelling, using clear sentences including the question and the answer.

- All children can improve their retelling by:

> o **Drawing a story map or story board before writing.**
>
> o **Telling their version to a partner before writing to check that it flows.**
>
> o **Having actions to link the question words to their meaning.**
>
> o **Trying out questions in role-play so they understand how to use them.**
>
> o **Answering questions.**
>
> o **Using a patterned question structure.**
>
> o **Playing games to practise questions, such as 'Twenty questions'.**

✏ EXTENDED WRITING

1 Shopping List

- Tell the children that you need to write a shopping list for some party food.

- Talk about the food that the children like to eat at parties. What do they like best. What do they dislike?

- Model writing each item on the list.

- Ask the children to draw the items on their list or attempt to write the words.

 Use Resource Sheet 8 on page 67 for children to create their shopping list.

2 Invitation to a party

- Act in role as a giant inviting the children to a fabulous feast. Tell the children when and where the party will be held and tell them what they should wear.

- Model composing an invitation to the giant's party. Can the children remember the details?

 Use Resource Sheet 9 on page 68 as a template for an invitation to the giant's party.

3 Postcard from a place you chose

- Display the pages with different locations and ask the children where they would choose to go on holiday.

- Orally rehearse some short sentences for a postcard from the destination the children have chosen.

 Use Resource Sheet 10 on page 69 to scribe a group postcard.

4 How to look after your pet

- Display the pages with the question 'Why not get yourself a pet …?' and discuss all the different types of animals the children can find.

- Choose one of the animals you would like to have as a class pet. Think of a name and talk about how you should look after it.

- Model writing some instructions on how to care for the class pet. Display the rules alongside an enlarged cut-out of the new class pet.

5 Big Book

- Make a class big book of the class version, including children's illustrations.

CROSS-CURRICULAR ACTIVITIES

Creating Dance and Music

- Create sound effects for one of the pages.

- Sing choosing and counting songs like *Ten in the Bed*.

Exploring Media and Materials

- Talk about the pictures of the characters on the family and friends pages. Tell the children that a picture of a person is called a portrait.

- Create a class gallery of self-portraits. Encourage the children to make funky frames for their portraits.

Knowledge and Understanding of the World

Time:

- Look at the different types of vehicles on the *'Would you travel ...'* pages. Work together to sort the vehicles into modern and old ones.

- You might like to create a timeline showing that the Roman chariot is older than the vintage car!

Place:

- Talk about the different clothes on the *'What would you wear?'* pages. Ask the children to choose clothes suitable for different types of weather.

- Ask the children to cut out or draw clothes to take to the beach on a sunny day and for a farm trip in the autumn.

Design and making:

- Look at the different types of vehicles on the *'Would you travel ...'* pages. Sort the vehicles into different groups, such as two wheels, no wheels, flying, etc.

- Design and make junk model vehicles that float or have wheels.

Exploration and investigation:

- Group the different types of food on the pages *'When you got hungry, what would you eat?'* into categories such as party food, vegetables, fruit, etc.

Problem Solving, Reasoning and Numeracy

Numbers as labels and for counting:

- Go through the book playing a counting game by asking questions such as: *Can you find me five treats for a princess?*, *Can you find me three hats for your mum?*

Physical development

Using equipment and materials:

- Give the children equipment to choose from such as hoops, bean bags, skipping ropes, balls, mats, etc.

- Tell them they can choose three pieces of equipment to make a racing game.

Personal Social and Emotional Development

Making relationships:

- Display the pages about jobs and talk about some of the different jobs.

- Ask the children: *Is there a job you'd like to do?*

- Ask the children to take turns to mime which job they would like for the rest of the group to guess.

Role-play area

- Provide collections of toys, e.g. animals, people, vehicles for play.

- Ask: *If you could choose an animal, which would you choose?* The child replies: *I would choose...*

- Extend this by giving reasons for the choice and using the word 'because'.

Check out the *Stories for Writing* Planning CD-ROM for week-by-week literacy plans, exciting cross-curricular ideas and extra resource sheets.

My Brother

 TALK

- Before reading the book, ask the children to think about who is in their family or who cares for them. Talk about ages – who is older or younger than them?

- Encourage the children to talk about what they like doing with their family, games they like playing and places they like visiting.

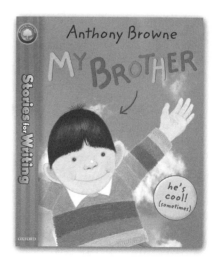

Use Resource Sheet 1 on page 70 for children to draw a picture of themselves and their family. They may wish to add extra details of family pets or activities.

 READ

1 Read the story together

- Select *My Brother* on the CD-ROM.

- Click on *Read* to listen to the story being read from beginning to end without interruption.

- Enjoy the story and let the children discuss any aspect they are interested in.

- Let the children raise their own questions.

2 Book Talk

- Reread the story and make sure it is on display whilst you explore these open questions. Make this session exciting and dynamic by encouraging paired and group discussions and interact with the text using the zoom, sticky notes and annotating tools to record the children's responses and ideas.

  - *What do you like about the boy?*
  - *Can you find something that isn't labelled in the pictures and talk about it?*
  - *Do you think he can really do all these things? Why/why not?*
  - *What do you think is the coolest thing that he can do?*

- Talk about the pictures.

- Stop at points in the book and ask:

  - *What do you notice on this page?*
  - *What is clever about this page?*
  - *What other words could you use instead of cool on this page?*
  - *What story does this character come from?*
  - *What sort of stories do you think he has read?*
  - *What words would you use to describe what he's doing here?*

 Use Resource Sheet 2 on page 71 for children to note a personal response to the story.

3 Explore the story

Setting: He's a great jumper

● Use the zoom tool to look at the hidden elephants under the jumping boy and ask: *How do you think the elephants are feeling?*

● Ask the children: *Where is the boy climbing?* Use the zoom tool to explore the cityscape and to reveal the blonde braided hair to the left of the boy. Ask the children: *Where do you think the boy is climbing to?*

● Zoom in on the gorilla and the lady and ask: *What might they be thinking?* Encourage the children to give reasons for their answers.

 Use Resource Sheet 3 on page 73 to talk about other places for the brother to climb.

Characters: bullies

● Turn to the pages with the bully and monster and ask: *What might the brother be saying to the bully?*

● Click on the speech and thought bubbles in the toolbar and drag them to the brother and the bully. Ask: *What might the bully be thinking?* Scribe the children's suggestions.

● Repeat the process, asking: *What might the brother and monster be feeling?*

Word and Language Games: describing words (adjectives)

● Choose different spreads and model using describing words: a *stripy jumper*, *spiky hair*, *sharp fangs*, *scary eyes*, etc.

● Now encourage the children to suggest other adjectives.

● Remember – they do not have to know what an adjective is, but they should be encouraged to use them!

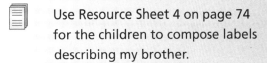 Use Resource Sheet 4 on page 74 for the children to compose labels describing my brother.

● **Game: What's in the box?** Show the children a box. Lift the lid and react to what you see. Describe what's inside using adjectives and ask the children to guess. (You might describe a toy monster as *furry*, *ferocious*, *red* or *green-striped*, *googly-eyed*.) Place other objects in the box for children to describe to the class.

Role-play and Drama

● Look at the picture of the cool cat. Ask the children which animal they would like to be. Ask them to mime being that animal. Can the class work out which animal they are?

● Hot-seat the brother and encourage children to ask questions to find out more about him.

4 Guided/group and independent reading

● You will find ideas for parents/carers to use *My Brother* with their child at home on the inside front cover of the storybook.

● You will find ideas for guided/group reading using *My Brother* on the inside back cover of the storybook.

An extract from *My Brother*, by Anthony Browne, with kind permission from Random House Children's Books

MY BROTHER

READ

5 Reading as a Writer

Return to the book and use it to explore the questions below, beginning to think about what might be needed to create your own version.

Plot

● Discuss with the children the kind of story *My Brother* is. It is all about one character. It makes lists of what someone is good at.

● *What other things might the brother be good at*? (For example, adding up, skipping, cooking, etc.)

Setting

● *Where else could the brother play football?* He could play football at school, on the beach, in the garden.

● *Where could he fly to?* He could fly to school, he could fly to the shops, he could fly to the other side of the world!

● *Where else could he skateboard?* In the park, at school, in the garden.

Character

● *Who is the main character?* The brother is the main character.

● Tell the children to imagine they are going to write about my sister, my mum, my dad or my friend. *What might we change in the story?*

Language

● Reread the story. *Are there any other words that could be used instead of cool?* (For example, *fantastic, brilliant, super, fabulous, wonderful, great*, etc.)

6 Other stories to read

Family stories

○ *Stan and His Gran* by Sarah Garland

○ *The Second Princess* by Tony Ross

○ *The Trouble with… (Mum, Dad, Gran and Grandad series)* by Babette Cole

○ *My Dad, My Mum* and *Zoo* by Anthony Browne

Stories written and illustrated by Anthony Browne

○ *Silly Billy*

○ *Things I like*

○ *Look what I've got*

7 Links to Oxford Reading Tree classic stories Stages 1–2

● Lists: *I See* (Stage 1), *Shopping* (Stage 1), *Kipper's Diary* (Stage 1+)

● Family Members: *Who Is It?* (Stage 1), *Floppy, Floppy* (Stage 1), *Get Dad* (Stage 1), *Hello Grandma* (Stage 1+), *Good Old Mum* (Stage 1+)

● Fun Activities: *The Pancake* (Stage 1), *Fun at the Beach* (Stage 1), *Go On, Mum* (Stage 1+), *The Toys Party* (Stage 2), *The Water Fight* (Stage 2)

TELL

1 Imitate: *My Brother*

- The children need to fully understand and internalise the story before they move on to telling Pie's simple innovated story.

- Try to embed some of the key phrases and patterned language so the children are familiar with the story structure and repeated phrases.

- Emphasise the verbs as you retell the story, to highlight what my brother is doing.

- Pick up on key phrases about my brother, such as *He's really cool, my brother; He can run so fast that he can fly; And guess what, I'm cool too!*

- If appropriate, use an enlarged copy of the *My Brother* story map on Resource Sheet 5 for children to retell the story in their own words, or draw your own.

 Use Resource Sheet 5 on page 74 to retell *My Brother* as a class.

2 Simple patterned innovation: Pie Corbett's story

- Tell the class that they are going to learn how to tell a new story, *My Friend*. It is similar to *My Brother*, but some things have changed.

- At this level, the simple patterned language of the sentences makes the story structure very predictable. Only very simple changes are made, such as names, adjectives and verbs, which slot perfectly into the original sentence structure.

- Click on *Tell* to play the video of Pie Corbett telling the story of *My Friend* using his story map and actions. Encourage the class to join in.

- Replay the video a number of times. As the children become more confident, gradually turn down the volume so that they retell the story without Pie's voice.

- Ask the children to retell the story as a class, then in groups or pairs, before they have a go on their own.

- Retelling is not a memory game. Most children will need to see a story map, do the actions and possibly use objects, to retell the story clearly.

- An enlarged photocopy of the story map, or your own version of it, should always be displayed.

 Use Resource Sheet 6 on page 75 for children to use to retell *My Friend*. Some children may want to create their own story maps. Resource Sheet 7 on page 76 shows Pie's story script.

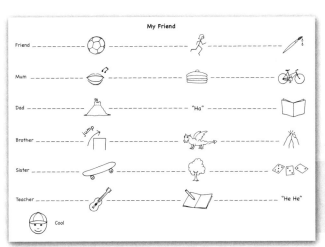

A story map of Pie's simple innovated story, *My Friend*

WRITE

1 Planning together

- Click on *Write* to use Pie's story map to help you create a shared, simple innovated class story.

- Make simple changes and practise each one as you add them to the story map on screen or on a flip chart. In this way your own version of the story will gradually develop.

- Ensure the children are involved in this process, using partner talk to make up their ideas.

- Ideas for changes include:

  o Change the main character, e.g. my friend, my sister, my teacher.

  o Add new activities, e.g. they could be good at swimming, snorkelling or drumming.

  o Add different adjectives, e.g. super, fabulous, wonderful.

2 Shared writing

- As well as simple changes, try adding in extra details to embellish the story. This could be 'dropping in' words (adjectives) or adding whole sentences and chunks of text.

- Once the children know the new class story, move into shared writing.

  o Focus on the things that each character is good at. Model orally composing a list of activities each character is good at. Use actions and drawings to help the children remember the activities on the list.

  o Ask the children to talk to their partner about what the characters could be good at. Take some of their ideas and use them in the shared story.

3 Recording children creating their own stories

- Lead children through developing their own map based on this story.

- In pairs, encourage them to tell and retell their version before recording it.

- Work with groups, pairs or individual children to help them record stories at their own level.

Children can:

o dictate to an adult who scribes

o record their story using a microphone

o video their story with a digital camera

o perform to a group

o create their own mark-making

o attempt writing.

WRITE

4 Guided writing

Focus: begin to use captions and simple sentences sometimes using punctuation (EYF CCL Writing scale point 8)

- This session should occur once the children have composed some of their story (orally, scribed or written).

- Look at a section of the shared story (for example, *My Mum is really cool. She can jump up high*). Read it aloud together. Ask the children to think how they could improve the second sentence. *What else might Mum be good at?*

- Ask the children to work with their partner to come up with a sentence that describes what Mum is good at. Model writing the final sentence on the whiteboard. Draw the children's attention to the basic punctuation as you write.

- Give the children time to draw a picture and copy their final sentence. Some children may wish to make some different word choices.

- You can differentiate this session for less confident and more confident children.

  ○ Work as a group to compose simple sentences about Mum, which you scribe as a group text.

  ○ Challenge children to try to write their own sentences about what Mum is good at.

5 Assessing children's writing

Focus: begin to use captions and simple sentences sometimes using punctuation (EYF CCL Writing scale point 8)

- Focus on the children's control of the sentence. Does it follow the pattern you have been using? Are any variations effective? Does it contain all the information? Whether recorded orally or in writing, confident writers will include a variety of ideas that are not jumbled, but well thought through. Less confident children will have difficulty holding all their ideas in order.

- Record children's ability and confidence in saying sentences aloud or in writing and inventing interesting ideas.

- All children can improve their sentences by:

  ○ Drawing a story map or story board before writing.

  ○ Telling their story to a partner before writing to check it flows.

  ○ Having visual prompts to help them during their retelling.

  ○ Practising orally until they are confident with each sentence.

  ○ Having their sentences read or said back to them so they can hear if they make sense.

  ○ Being confident of what they want to write before they attempt to scribe anything.

MY BROTHER

✎ EXTENDED WRITING

1 Cool Characters and Brilliant Books

- Display the storybook character page. Ask the children to look at the characters behind my brother. Can they identify who they are?

- Talk about the type of books that each of the characters might come from.

- Work together to compile a list of characters and books for a 'Cool Characters and Brilliant Books' display.

2 You're super cool because...

- Ask the children if they can remember some of the things that the brother is great at.

- Ask each child in the group to think of something they enjoy doing and ask them to share this with the group.

- Now ask each member of the group to think of a positive thing to say about the other members of the group.

 Use Resource Sheet 8 on page 77 to create badges for each child in the group, showing what they are good at.

3 Helping hands

- Display the pages with the bully and talk about times when children might want help at school.

- Ask the children to talk with their partner to think about who can help them at school.

Use Resource Sheet 9 on page 78 to collect ideas about five people that the children can turn to when they are worried at school.

4 Important to me tree

- Display the final page of the story. Ask the children: *Who is important to you?*

- Discuss how families are made up of all sorts of people, relatives who are close or people who live far away. Can the children recall who is in their family?

- Talk about other people who might be important to us and could be included in a family tree. Children can draw or write the names of people who are important to them onto a tree. Use Resource Sheet 1 as a starting point.

5 People who help us

- Draw and paint large pictures of people who help us.

- Label the pictures with things they do and what we like about them.

- Add labels with arrows to describe their clothes.

6 Big Book

- Make a class big book of the class version including children's illustrations.

CROSS-CURRICULAR ACTIVITIES

Creating Dance and Music

- Look at the pages where the brother is a rock singer/disco dancer. Ask the children to think about the music they like to listen to and dance to.
- Make simple percussion instruments like shakers so that the children can make a rhythm. Invite the children to add their rhythm to songs and rhymes.
- Sing songs and rhymes about ourselves.

 Use Resource Sheet 10 on page 79 for examples of nursery rhymes to learn as a class.

Exploring Media and Materials

- Ask the children to design a really cool jumper for my brother to wear. They can use paints or collage to make it.

Knowledge and Understanding of the World

Time:
- Look at the picture of Anthony Browne's brother on the inside page. Ask the children: *Do you think Anthony Browne's brother still looks like this? How might he have changed?*
- Ask the children to bring in pictures of themselves when they were babies and discuss how they have changed.

Place:
- Display the pages where my brother is a terrific climber and ask the children to talk about what they can see.
- Encourage the children to think of activities they could do in a city or in the countryside.
- Make a list of the activities that you could do in the different places and ask the children which they would like to visit.

Design and making:
- Display the pages where my brother can fly and ask the children to talk about what they can see. Tell the children that my brother needs a flying outfit.
- Can the children design and make a cape for the brother?

Exploration and investigation:
- Explore different materials and their properties to decide what would make the best jumper.
- Decide as a group the criteria for a good jumper (warm, soft, easy to put on, etc) and use these to judge the different materials.

Problem Solving, Reasoning and Numeracy

Shape, space and measures:
- Use unifix, blocks or beads on a thread to create patterns of two colours asking the children to predict what the next colour will be.
- Ask children to create patterns of two or three-coloured blocks.

Physical development

Movement and space:
- Play ball games that involve kicking and passing in small groups.

Personal Social and Emotional Development

Making relationships:
- Use circle time games to help children learn each other's names and facts about each other, such as their likes and dislikes.

Role-play area

- Display family pictures or pictures of people who are close to the children.
- Use dolls and toys of people to play at 'families' – provide small furniture.

MY BROTHER

Check out the *Stories for Writing* Planning CD-ROM for week-by-week literacy plans, exciting cross-curricular ideas and extra resource sheets.

Name ....

Wild and farm animals

Wild animals	Farm animals

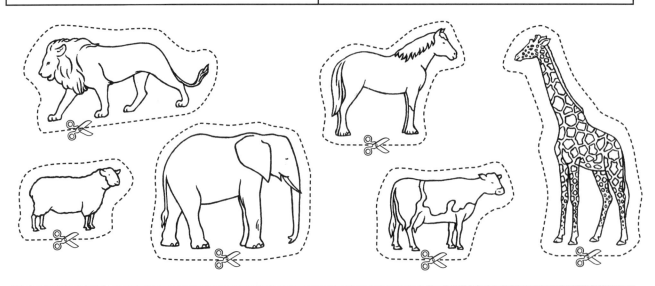

o Talk about which animals can be farmed and which are wild.

o Help the children to cut the animals out and stick them into the correct column.

o Discuss where else they may see the wild animals.

Name ....

Rosie's Walk

Draw Rosie back at home on her nest.

How is Rosie feeling now? Talk with your partner.

Draw what you think happened to the fox in the end.

Draw the animal you liked best in the story.

o Ask children to complete a personal response to the story.

o Encourage children to discuss their ideas with a partner.

Name ....

How did I do?

Hen mask

○ Encourage children to colour in their masks.

○ Help them to cut the masks out and cut around the holes to thread string through.

○ Act as a narrator and get the children to use the hen and fox masks to act out *Rosie's Walk* in pairs.

Name ....

Fox mask

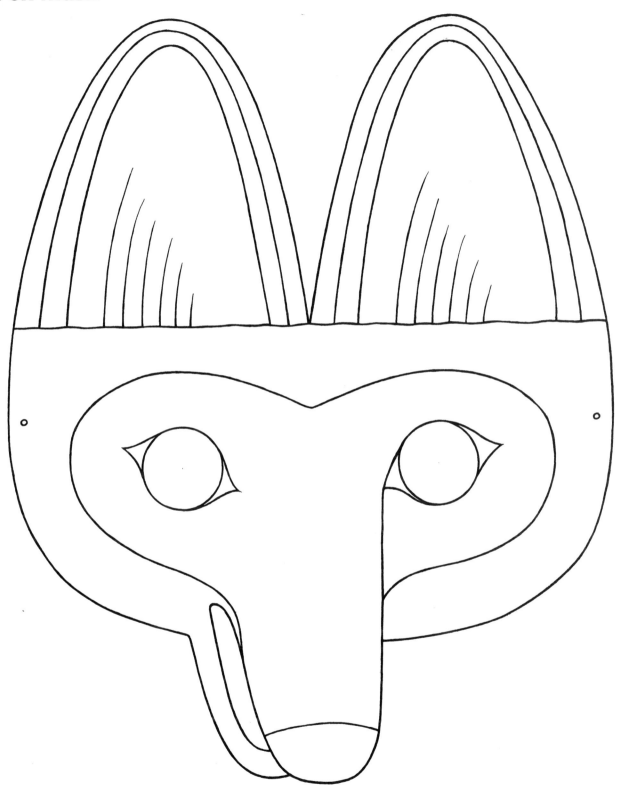

○ Encourage children to colour in their masks.

○ Help them to cut the masks out and cut around
   the holes to thread string through.

○ Act as a narrator and get the children to use the
   hen and fox masks to act out *Rosie's Walk* in pairs.

Story map for *Rosie's Walk*

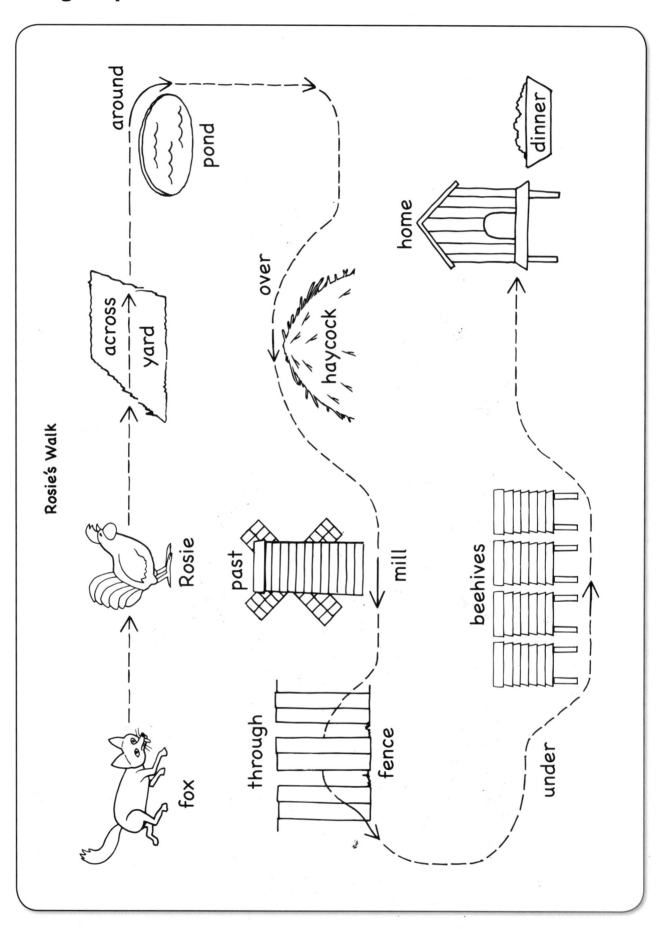

o This is a story map for *Rosie's Walk*. Display an enlarged version in the classroom as you retell the story.

Pie's story map

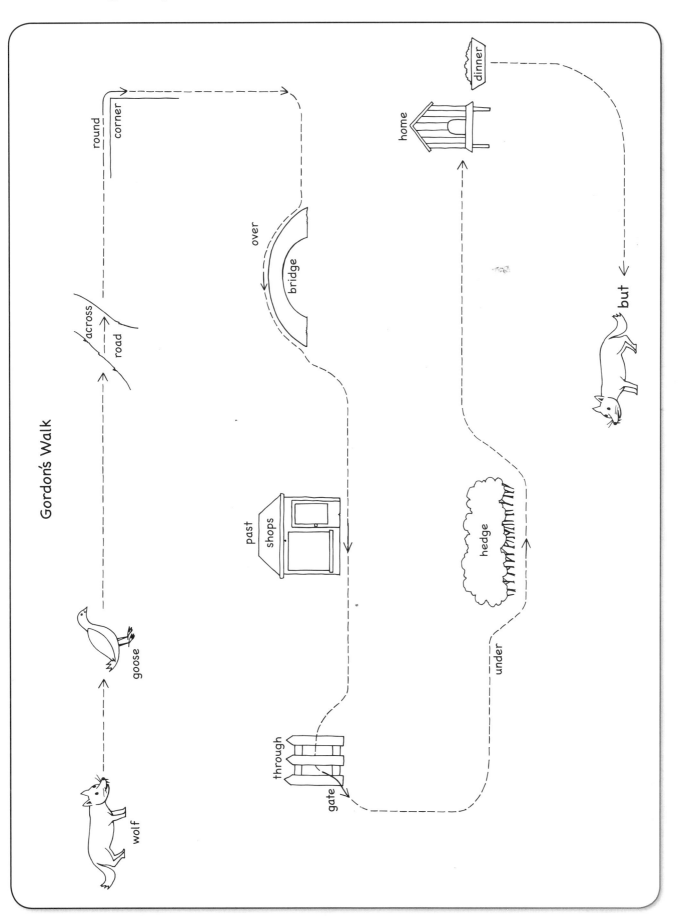

○ Display this story map in the classroom when the children are ready to join in retelling Pie's innovated story.

Gordon's Walk

Gordon the Goose went for a walk,
but a wolf followed him!

First, he went across the road,
but a wolf followed him!

Next, he went around the corner,
but a wolf followed him!

After that, he went over the bridge,
but a wolf followed him!

Then, he went past the shops,
but a wolf followed him!

Later on, he went through a gate,
but a wolf followed him!

Finally, he went under the hedge,
but a wolf followed him!

In the end, he got back home just
in time for dinner…
but the wolf went home hungry!

○ Use this script to help you lead the children in retelling *Gordon's Walk*.

Name ....

Wanted!

....

....

....

o Orally compose a sentence to describe the fox. Print an enlarged copy of this Resource Sheet and scribe the shared sentence onto it.

o Photocopy your scribed poster for the children to add to. Ask them to draw the fox in the space above.

Name ....

All about chickens

| beak | feet | hen | chicks |

Hens	....
Chicks	....
Eggs	....

o Read the labels and check the children understand them.

o Enlarge the Resource Sheet and work with the children to label the picture correctly.

o Work together to orally compose a sentence for each heading and then scribe it for the group.

Name ....

A trip to the farm

....

∽ Farm ∽

Price (adult) £ ....

Price (child) £ ....

Opening times ....

○ Talk about what information may appear on a ticket to a farm, such as the name, opening times, price, etc. Model filling in a ticket as a group activity.

○ Encourage the children to complete their own tickets using the class model, and to colour in the pictures of farm animals.

Name ....

What would you choose?

What did you eat for breakfast?

What is in your school bag?

What book are you reading?

○ Talk about the choices the children made this morning.   ○ Ask the children to draw their choices in the boxes.

Name ....

You Choose

My friend...

My home...

My clothes...

My pet...

- Ask children to complete a personal response to the story.
- Encourage children to discuss ideas with a partner.
- Ask the children to draw their choices in the spaces above.

My storybook characters

Which character would you choose for a fairytale story?

Which character would you choose for a scary story?

Which character would you choose for your story?

○ Turn to the family and friends pages.

○ Ask the children to choose characters for each of the questions above and draw them in the spaces.

Name ....

A secret door

A secret door. What could be on the other side?

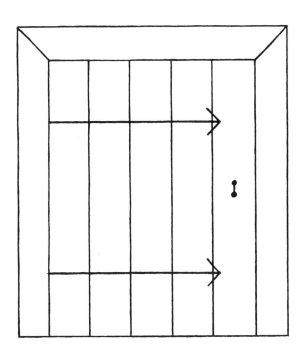

o Talk about what might be behind the secret door.

o Ask the children to colour in the door and then use the space above to draw or stick what they think could be behind it.

o Help children to cut out the door and stick it over their picture so that when they open it, it reveals what's behind.

Story map for *You Choose*

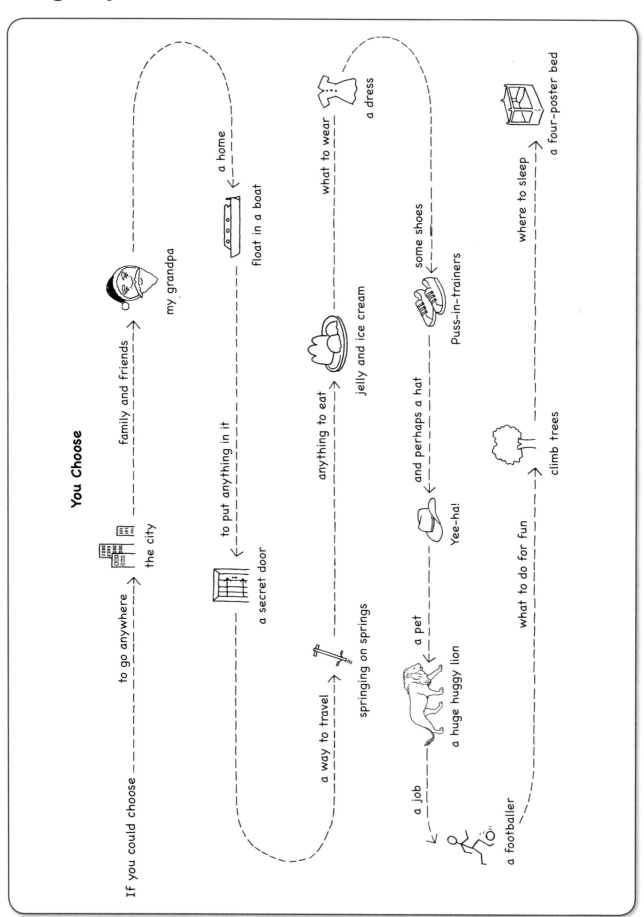

You Choose

If you could choose

to go anywhere

the city

family and friends

my grandpa

a secret door

to put anything in it

float in a boat

a home

a way to travel

springing on springs

anything to eat

jelly and ice cream

what to wear

a dress

a job

a pet

a huge huggy lion

and perhaps a hat

Yee-ha!

some shoes

Puss-in-trainers

a footballer

what to do for fun

climb trees

where to sleep

a four-poster bed

○ This is a story map for *You Choose*. Display an enlarged version in the classroom as you retell the story.

Pie's story map

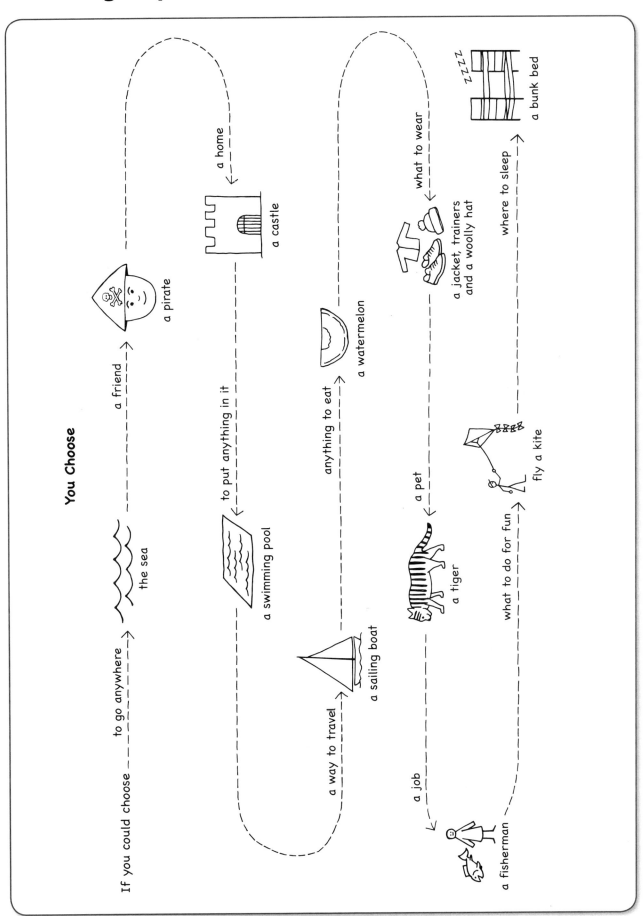

You Choose

If you could choose — to go anywhere → the sea

a friend → a pirate

to go anywhere

a way to travel → a sailing boat

to put anything in it → a swimming pool

anything to eat → a watermelon

a home → a castle

a job → a fisherman

a pet → a tiger

what to do for fun → fly a kite

what to wear → a jacket, trainers and a woolly hat

where to sleep → a bunk bed

zzzz

○ Display this story map in the classroom when the children are ready to join in retelling Pie's innovated story.

You Choose

If you could choose to go anywhere,
where would you choose?
I would choose to go to the sea.

If you could choose a friend,
who would you choose?
I would choose a pirate.

If you could choose a house to live in,
where would you choose?
I would choose a castle.

If you could choose to put anything in it,
what would you choose?
I would choose a swimming pool.

If you could choose a way to travel,
what would you choose?
I would choose a sailing boat.

If you could choose anything to eat,
what would you choose?
I would choose a juicy water melon.

If you could choose what to wear,
what would you choose?
I would choose a warm jacket, some
trainers and a woolly hat.

If you could choose a pet,
what would you choose?
I would choose a tiger.

If you could choose any job,
what would you choose?
I would choose to be a fisherman.

If you could choose to do anything for fun,
what would you choose?
I would fly a kite.

If you could choose where to sleep,
where would you sleep?
I would choose a bunk bed.

Goodnight!

○ Use this script to help you lead the children in retelling *You Choose*.

Name ....

Party shopping list

o Ask the children to draw the items on their list, or attempt to write the words.

Name ....

A giant's party

Please come to my party!

Who

....

When

....

Where

....

Time

....

RSVP

○ Talk about the giant's party – where might it be held, on what day of the week and at what time of day?

○ Ask the children to fill in their invitations, using your scribed version as a model.

○ Make a post box for children to post their invitations.

Name ....

Where would you go on holiday?

....

....

....

....

○ Look at the first pages of *You Choose* showing different destinations.

○ Ask the children where they would choose to go on holiday.

○ Orally rehearse some short sentences for a postcard from the destination the children have chosen and then work as a group to fill in the template above.

Name ....

My family

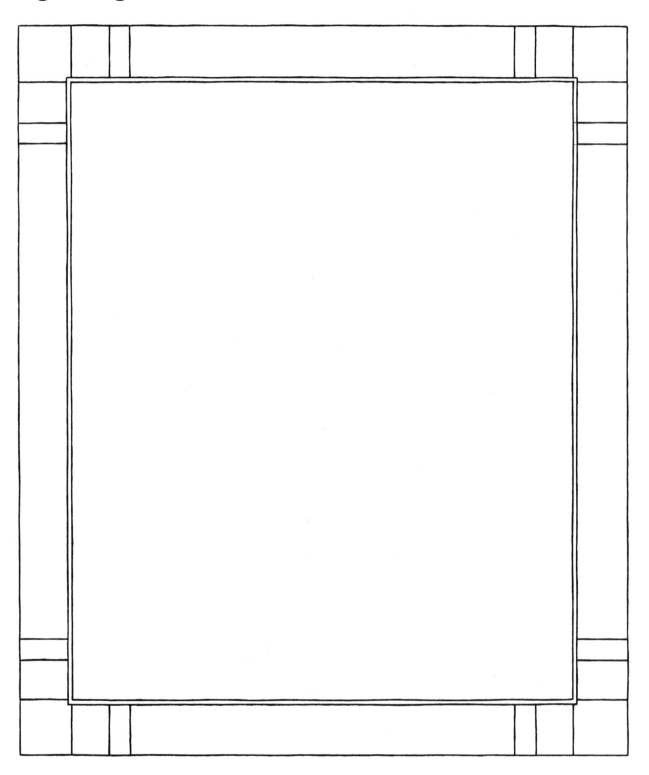

○ Ask the children to draw a picture of themselves and their family.

○ Help them to label the pictures.

○ They may wish to add extra details such as family pets or family activities.

Name ....

My Brother

What do you think is the best thing the brother can do?

What do you think is the coolest thing about him?

 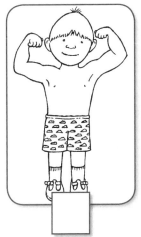 

Draw what is cool about you.

○ Ask children to complete a personal response to the story.

○ Read through the questions with the children and encourage them to discuss their ideas with a partner.

Name ....

A terrific climber

o Talk about the different pictures and whether the children think it would be fun, scary or dangerous to climb these different places.

o Ask the children to circle the face which shows what they think about the brother climbing these different places.

Name ....

My brother is cool

o Ask the children to describe the different parts of the brother, for example super shoes, etc.

o Encourage children to orally compose labels for the picture, using adjectives.

o Scribe their ideas or support them in writing labels.

Story map for *My Brother*

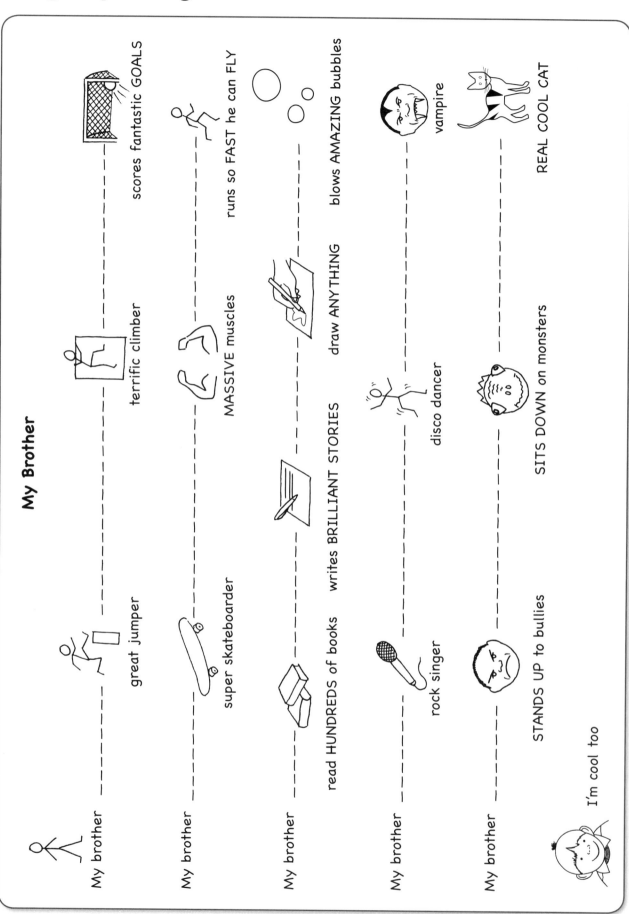

My Brother

My brother — great jumper · terrific climber · scores fantastic GOALS

My brother — super skateboarder · MASSIVE muscles · runs so FAST he can FLY

My brother — read HUNDREDS of books · writes BRILLIANT STORIES · draw ANYTHING · blows AMAZING bubbles

My brother — rock singer · disco dancer · vampire

My brother — STANDS UP to bullies · SITS DOWN on monsters · REAL COOL CAT

I'm cool too

o This is a story map for *My Brother*. Display an enlarged version in the classroom as you retell the story.

Pie's story map

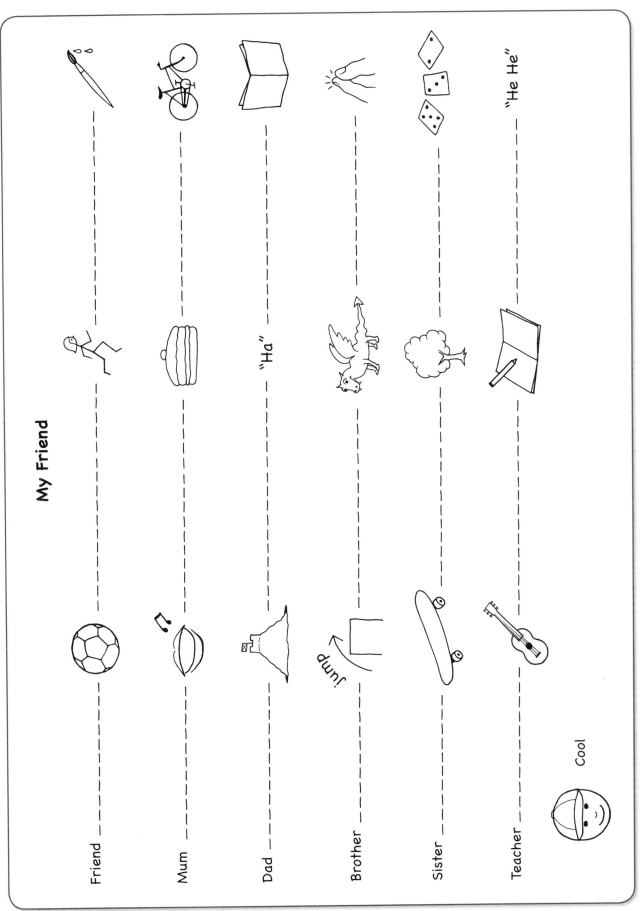

o Display this story map in the classroom when the children are ready to join in retelling Pie's innovated story.

My Friend

My friend is really cool.
She can kick a football, run really fast
and paint pictures.

My mum is really cool.
She can sing pop songs, bake a cake
and ride on a bicycle.

My dad is really cool.
He can build sandcastles, tell good jokes
and reads us stories.

My brother is really cool.
He can jump high, draw amazing dragons
and click his fingers.

My sister is really cool.
She can ride on a skateboard, climb up trees
and play cards.

My teacher is really cool.
She can play the guitar, write funny stories
and makes us laugh.

And guess what...
I'm cool too!
How about you?

○ Use this script to help you lead the children in retelling *My Friend*.

Name ....

How did I do?

Badges for my friends

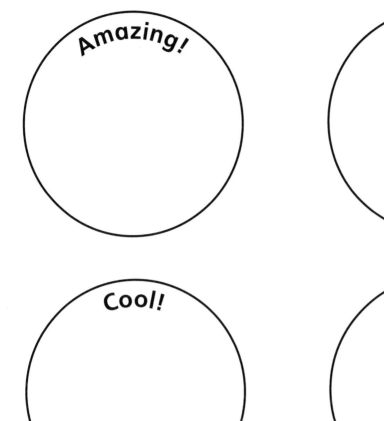

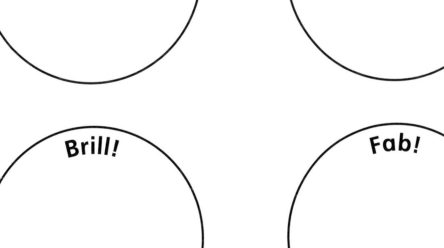

○ In small groups, ask each child to think of a positive thing to say about the other members of the group.

○ Ask them to make badges for each other. They can draw a picture to show what the other children are good at.

This may be reproduced for class use within purchaser's institution

Name ....

' _____ 's Helping Hand'

When I am worried I can get help from...

1 ....

2 ....

3 ....

4 ....

5 ....

o Ask the children to talk with their partner about who can help them at school if they are worried about something.

o Work with small groups to help the children complete their own 'Helping hand'. They can decorate them and display them in the classroom.

Name ....

Nursery rhymes

Just me

Eight pink fingers standing up tall,
Two little ears to hear mummy call;
One little nose that I can blow,
Ten pink toes all in a row.
Two little thumbs that wiggle up and down;
Two little feet to stamp on the ground;
Hands to clap and eyes to see,
What fun it is to be just me!

Ten fingers

I have ten fingers   *(hold up both hands, fingers spread)*
And they all belong to me.   *(point to self)*
I can make them do things,
Would you like to see?

I can shut them up tight,   *(make fists)*
I can open them wide,   *(open hands)*
I can put them together,   *(place palms together)*
I can make them all hide,   *(put hands behind back)*

I can make them jump high,   *(hands over head)*
I can make them jump low,   *(touch floor)*
I can fold them up quietly,   *(fold hands in lap)*
And hold them just so.

o Enlarge copies of these nursery rhymes and learn them as a class.

Notes